May you fully
LIV2DAY!

♡,

Dr. Paula McDonald

PRAISE FOR *LIV2DAY*

From the first day Paula told me about her concept of Theosynthesis, I have been intrigued to hear more about it. She has such an uncomplicated way of explaining how the whole person (body, soul, and spirit) ties to God. When Paula began a Bible study, I looked forward to hearing more of her Theosynthesis ideas. I have to say the biggest influence Paula's teaching has had on me is learning how to really dig into the Bible, finding interesting historical facts, seeing how science fits into the Bible, and how we can apply it personally. Thank you, Paula, for inspiring me to always be learning.

—ANN BLESSING. EXECUTIVE

Dr. McDonald challenged me to take a heart journey, unlike anything I have experienced before. She embraces a biblical, holistic view of the connection of mind, body, and Spirit - Theosynthesis.

SARAH OLSON, MASTER OF ARTS IN CHRISTIAN SCHOOL EDUCATION

I appreciate Paula's passion for teaching & the depth of her research. She has a unique ability to keep a room full of women engaged & excited about what she is sharing.

—SARA GALVAN, RETIRED EDUCATOR

I love the strength, wisdom, and sensitivity God has given Paula. Her passion and excitement have enticed me to go deeper in my relationship with God and his word. When Father God touches you, you will never be the same. Through personal stories and her presence, you can feel God's hand at work. Thank you, Paula, for helping us all to see God as you see Him.

—MICHELLE SHELTON, PHILANTHROPIST,
AND RETIRED PHARMACEUTICAL SALES AND SPEECH PATHOLOGIST, BSE

Paula is my Proverb 27:9. My Christian friend in Christ combing gracious acts of kindness, wise advice, words of encouragement and friendly counsel with the gospel of Christ in order to improve and encourage my spiritual growth.

—ROBBIE GAFFIN COOK, PROFESSIONAL CORPORATE TRAVEL EXECUTIVE

THEOSYNTHESIS®

LIV2DAY

Abundantly Connecting to God

DR. PAULA MCDONALD

BOSS

MEDIA

Distributed globally by Boss Media.
New York | Los Angeles | London | Sydney

Hardcover ISBN: 978-1-63337-402-7
E-book ISBN: 978-1-63337-403-4
Library of Congress Control Number: 2020940545

Manufactured and printed in the United States of America

I could not have completed this work without the support from my wonderful husband Mark. Also, thank you to our dear friends, Dr. Gordon and Cherise Selley who allowed me to escape to their beautiful Destin home to finish this project.

To all of you who have encouraged me, your support means the world! Thank you dear friends and family members who have joined me on this exciting journey!

Cayden, my little buddy, and side-kick. You have enriched our lives immensely. I thank God for you each and every day! Always remember to continue to grow strong in the Lord and live your life fully every moment.

To my EXHALE Bible Discovery Group, I love each of you so very much. You have allowed me to share tidbits about this book and each of you has poured into me with your love, support, and trust.

Finally, thank you to Dr. David Bush who encouraged me to finish my doctoral studies!

TO MY WONDERFUL TEAM

These special women enabled this project to go from a concept to reality. Thank you to each one of you for your leadership, your creativity, and your support. I am blessed to know and work with you all.

Michelle Robinson - Publisher
Sherrie Clark - Editor / Project Manager
Emily Hitchcock - Designer

"To this end I labor, struggling with all His energy, which so powerfully works in me."
Colossians 1:29

CONTENTS

INTRODUCTION

YOU PICKED UP this book for a reason. Before you make any decisions about this book, let me encourage you to read it with an open mind and an open heart. This book would not be here at all if I had closed my thoughts and not opened my mind to seeing things in a different light.

Many things shape our lives. Our families, upbringing, so-cio-economic status, education, religion, politics, trauma, illness, are just a few of the areas in life that form our character and personality.

I am a Christian. Let's get that right out there. As a Christian, I believe there is a God of the universe who creat-ed each one of us most uniquely and amazingly. God sent His Beloved Son, Jesus Christ, as a way of reaching down to us and have us pay attention.

I urge you, if your beliefs are different from mine, to continue reading this book with an open mind. Over the years, I have found that when I refuse to see or believe something, I am ultimately clos-ing myself off to potentially gleaning a new perspective. What have you got to lose?

Let me also state how or what others believe does not cause me to fear, pass judgment, or think poorly of anyone who holds a different belief or perspective from my own. We are each on our journey while on this earth. No matter where your journey has led you to this point, I ask that you allow yourself a moment to look deeply into your own heart and mind and consider the views I am about to share with you.

Could you stick with me as we explore this topic? I believe you too will find it fascinating and that it will perhaps provide you with a new way of thinking. I learned long ago to pay attention when I get that inkling, whisper, or gut-intuitive experience. Possessing a receptive learning style throughout my life has allowed me to engage with new information and ways of thinking. Ultimately, this learning style has shaped my life in extraordinary ways.

Theosynthesis came about from my passion for health and wellness, living toxin-free, and my firm belief in an Intelligent Designer—God. As I have discovered, trying to do anything in my life without acknowledging my Creator and giving Him credit, my life begins to spin out of control. Why is that?

My friends, this is what we are going to focus on and explore throughout this book. As I said before, your journey is yours, and what or how you think is ultimately up to you. No judgment and no condemnation. Just be open as you consider the thoughts presented here regarding Theosynthesis.

In a world of fast-paced, get-to-the-top, fitness-focused, beauty-focused, and "me, me, me," it is no wonder that we still find ourselves searching for more. We now have more information regarding health and fitness than ever before, yet so many people face more health challenges than ever. All the while, the information we need is right at our fingertips with the advent of the Internet. So why are we more unfit and sicker than ever before?

As I set out to write a curriculum for a wellness workshop I was conducting, I knew deep within my being that something significant was missing regarding the wellness industry. That something, however, is *the* most crucial facet of well-being. That something is God! As I pondered on this, I needed to create a diagram in which to explain what I knew God was pouring into me.

Every cycle on earth and within our own bodies is perfectly and precisely designed, each with its own precarious and delicate dance of equilibrium and balance.

With a degree in biology, the diagram of photosynthesis came to mind. The delicate cycle of sunlight and carbon dioxide is taken in by the plants, stored in the leaves as energy while putting out life-giving oxygen, and food is such a perfect and complete cycle. Everything, however, must be present within this cycle for it to function. In a diagram of photosynthesis, if just one aspect of this cycle were missing, it would be broken and would cease to function.

Science and the Bible have seemingly been in conflict with one another for a very long time. In both my science education as well as my Bible studies, I very clearly see evidence which points to an Intelligent Designer. Every cycle on earth and within our own bodies is perfectly and precisely designed, each with its own precarious and delicate dance of equilibrium and balance. When one tiny thing is off, things go awry.

We will dig into both science and God in much greater depth in the following chapters of this book. There are so many exciting discoveries as man continues in his quest for knowledge. The more I learn of science and the Bible, the more I know beyond a shadow of a doubt, there is a God of the universe who is in complete control!

Now, back to the topic of Theosynthesis. I am thrilled to share this revelation. When we open ourselves up and connect with the Almighty God, He will show us more than we could ever imagine. Buckle up as we embark on this exciting knowledge quest.

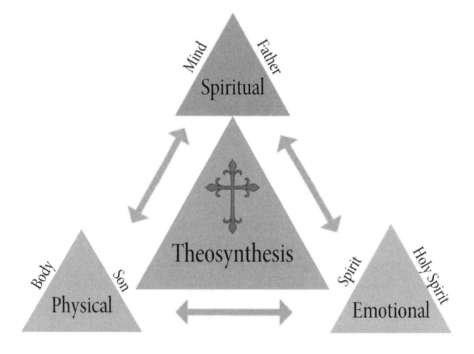

With everything in life, there will be people who will choose not to see the truth in this or any concept. That is fine. As I mentioned before, they are on their journey as you and I are on ours. For many, learning something new may alter the way they think. A concept they have long-believed now becomes challenged, causing fear and even anxiety. Science, however, has long been known for being open to new thoughts and ideas.

There needs to be no fear. Fear is an unpleasant emotion caused by the belief that someone or something is dangerous and likely to cause pain or a threat. There is no harm in taking a look at something in an entirely different way. It's certainly not dangerous, nor will it be a threat to your safety or cause you pain.

The only threat in seeking out new information lies in the possible result of rethinking a secure belief system. Join me as we explore a few concepts with a different approach. This information may challenge both Christians and non-Christians. Being challenged is entirely okay. There is no harm in digging deep and opening your mind to new information.

This book will not read like a novel. You may choose to skip ahead and read the chapters of this book in a random fashion. How you read through this book isn't the main point; what you get out of it is what is essential. Take your time to read, reread, digest, and make notes as you study this book.

The fear of the LORD is the beginning of knowledge;
Fools despise wisdom and instruction (Proverbs 1:7).

THEOSYNTHESIS®

PART I
UNDERSTANDING GOD

CHAPTER 1

WHO IS GOD?

TO FULLY GRASP the concepts outlined in this book, it will be essential first to understand who God is. Without a firm distinction of God, what I am referring to would result in confusion and false information. There are many definitions and beliefs regarding God. Therefore, I will outline the God that I have come to know.

Let me say for the record, the God I know has guided me through a deeply personal journey. In addition to my own experiences and testimony, I've also dedicated the last 20 years immersing myself in profound studies of the Scriptures. My faith has been more solidified as I have become an ardent student of the Bible.

Isn't it interesting how many people refute the Bible, yet they have never really studied it? It's easy to pick up a book and read through it simply; however, comprehending the text takes a lot more research, questioning, and dedication. My desire to dig down and understand the Scriptures has led me on a quest for where I am today in my belief system. Consequently, this project has evolved due to earnest studying and an immersion into the Bible.

My study of the Bible led me to a deeper understanding that God is the One and only true God. He is *the* God of Isaac, Jacob, and Israel. He is the God of the universe and created all things. He alone is the God of the Holy Bible.

In fact, as a student of science, the more I have studied and learned about the Bible, the more I recognize how it all points to an all-knowing perfect Creator. We are not just random molecules and cells that just happened to arrange together correctly by chance over millions of years. This particular theory takes a great deal more faith than believing in an intelligent designer—God.

In religions around the world, many refer to a belief in a supreme being. Humans, inexplicably, are wired to seek a higher power. It's as if down within our very core, we were created to seek out God. Because we were designed and wired to know Him deep within our genetic DNA code, God created man with His imprint within our genes. We will explore this topic in-depth in Chapter 38.

As history has shown, there has been much conflict and bloodshed as a result of man's quest to seek God. Today, there are still horrific wars with the main point of controversy centering on religion or of God. The subject of God has brought appalling tension and strife over the centuries. Why is this? Why would this one subject create such profound and divisive emotions?

For those who choose to follow the Christian faith, this book is written from the context of the One and only true God of the Holy Bible. This belief, however, is not just based on pure faith. The essence of our confidence in Him boils down to trust. Hope and faith indeed are difficult concepts, and we either have faith in God, or we have the belief that there is no God. Either belief system, however, requires faith.

Science has tried to deny Him. World leaders have tried to push Him out. Our modern world continues to feel threatened by Christians who claim to know the one true God.

Christians have and continue to be martyred all over the world for their belief in Jesus. How is it this one Gentleman creates so much tension? There is absolutely nowhere in the Bible or any other historical document that teaches Jesus was a terrible person. Quite the contrary; He was known as humble, loving, and gracious.

How then can there be this much strife over someone who many claim does not exist or was not the person He said He was? Do you know of any other subject which has caused this much confusion, hate, power, and conflict? There just has to be something then to this God and this Jesus!

Man has always desired to know things. Being wired to have a desire to discover, seek, and find is inherently in our DNA. There is nothing wrong with exploring new ways to think, believe, and comprehend. The problem lies in those who will look into the face of truth and yet still deny its existence simply because they cannot or will not choose to understand it.

Just because you don't understand something or don't choose to understand it does not make it an untruth. Being open to truth is the first step to fully understanding a new view. We may decide to close our minds to something, but it doesn't cause it to be untrue.

Let's take a look at the human emotion of love. There are no scientific tests to measure love, yet each one of us has experienced some form of love in our lives. For most of us, we will truly never fully understand love. Just because we don't understand it does not negate its existence.

One of my favorite verses in the Bible is Matthew 22:37. The Pharisees were questioning Jesus and trying to get Him to say something that would allow them to arrest him. They asked Him what they thought to be a trick question regarding what was the greatest commandment. Jesus replied:

> *"Love the Lord your God with all your heart and with all your soul and with all your <u>mind</u>."*

The word *mind* jumps out at me. God doesn't want us to accept things at face value. He desires us to question what we don't understand rather than merely making rash decisions about our beliefs. God is wise enough to tell us to *use* our minds. Think, evaluate, study, and research.

As I stated earlier, many question the validity of God or the Bible and have never even read or studied it. Reading something versus studying it are two entirely different things. I have read and studied the Bible from cover to cover; therefore, I've based my faith by using my mind and sound logic.

Of course, faith has a lot to do with my beliefs. Through my hope and many amazing experiences, God has allowed me to utilize my mind to discover even more truths about Him. A closed mind will never enable one to see God as He intended. What you choose to believe is a personal choice, and God will never force Himself on anyone.

Faith is a tough concept. Believing in something we cannot touch or see can be extremely difficult to accept. There are, however, many examples of faith in our everyday lives. As I stated before, just because something is hard to understand does not make it untrue.

Let's use the example of air. We cannot see it, yet we can see the effect it has on things around us. We observe trees moving in the wind, and we can feel the breeze on our skin. Science uses special instruments to measure the speed of air, thereby understanding the properties and characteristics of air.

The first law of physics states an object will remain at rest or in a steady state of motion unless an external force changes it.[1] As the wind blows, we see evidence of movement from those objects that are affected by the wind.

In trying to understand God, this is where many simply choose not to believe. Because they cannot see Him physically, they claim there is no God. Perhaps they cannot feel God, so they deny and dismiss Him. There are no scientific instruments to measure God; therefore, there are many claims He is not real.

Just as there are no instruments we can use to determine the existence of God, there is also no way to measure love or faith. Even without scientific evidence, we understand these forces to be viable and real. Belief in God then should not be dismissed just because He cannot be scientifically verified.

Isn't this just like man? We're so pompous in believing that because we cannot see, feel, or measure something, it doesn't exist. We are proud beings, and pride is often our biggest stumbling block. Ego is one of the biggest roadblocks to knowing God.

To openly assess any concept, one must be willing to see all sides of a subject. Therefore, what do we have to lose by exploring the idea of God? And, the bigger question is, what could you risk by denying God?

---

1 J.O. Smith, "Physical Audio Signal Processing," online book, 2010 edition, http://ccrma.stanford.edu/~jos/pasp/, Accessed May 2020.

Blaise Pascal, a French mathematician and philosopher, brilliantly wrote what is called, Pascal's Wager[2]: "*In order to try and come to the conclusion that God does exist through reason alone, the wise person should live their life as if there is a God. Doing so means that you have everything to gain (Heaven) and nothing to lose.*"

On the other side of the coin, however, Pascale wrote that "*If God doesn't exist, then we have lost nothing.*" Therefore, he wagered, saying basically, what have you got to lose by choosing to believe in God?

> ### Pascal's Wager
>
> "In order to try and come to the conclusion that God does exist through reason alone, the wise person should live their life as if there is a God. Doing so means that you have everything to gain (Heaven) and nothing to lose."
>
> "On the other side of the coin however, he wrote, that if God doesn't exist, then we have lost nothing." So he wagered saying basically, "What have you got to lose by choosing to believe in God?"

Blaise Pascal was and continues to be a highly respected scholar. His teachings are still revered and taught today. Being a brilliant man, he decisively came up with this wager that gives us much to think about and from which we can make informed decisions.

Reason alone, however, is not all that makes up the Christian faith. The root of the Christian faith is faith alone and acceptance of Christ, who died for our sins. Belief and faith go hand in hand. Apostle Paul taught in Romans 1:19–20 that knowing God is evident to all so that we as humans are without excuse.

"*Since what may be known about God is plain to them, because God has made it plain to them. For since the creation of the*

---

2   https://www.britannica.com/topic/Pascals-wager.

*world <u>God's invisible qualities</u> – His eternal power and divine
nature – have been clearly seen, being understood from what has
been made, so that men are without excuse."*

Did you see it? Right there in verse 20, we read about God's invisible qualities! He does have many qualities and attributes that are
not yet seen, and yet, we know them to be true. Just as human beings
have character traits we cannot see, such as thoughts and emotions,
we know they exist.

Knowing and understanding God is a lifelong adventure. He
is available to all who seek Him with an open heart and mind. He
chooses not to force His way into our lives but has provided a way
to know Him through the beautiful act of grace. We cannot earn
grace as it is merely a gift.

Grace means unmerited love. Unmerited means it cannot be
earned. Jesus, God's only Son, gave His life to humanity as a gift
of salvation. Additionally, we cannot earn this gift by anything we
do on our own. Our belief in and dedication to Jesus is a precious
gift of grace.

Many people stumble and stop right here at this profound
truth. They simply cannot grasp that a loving God would send His
only Son to die for sinful humankind. Through the simple act of
faith and acceptance, we become a part of His kingdom.

If you are one of those who have a difficult time with this concept, I urge you to honestly and openly search the Scriptures and ask
God for His guidance. I believe through the study of the Bible and
with an open heart, you will soon understand and be awed by the
concept of what grace truly means in your life.

As my stepfather was dying, I was at his bedside. For whatever reason, I found myself being the only one in the room. He was

barely breathing, and I could hear the whir of the oxygen tank. He began whispering.

I placed my ear close to him. "It's so simple, it's so simple," he repeated. I knew immediately he was seeing his Lord and Savior. Although he struggled with the concept of faith and grace, he saw first-hand how elementary it was. When you open your heart to God, He will show you how easy and yet how beautiful belief in Him can be.

We will never know all there is to know about God because we are not God. We have finite minds and can and never will be able to comprehend everything. We as prideful humans want to know all of the answers. People get hung up on concepts they don't understand and therefore refuse to be open. Close mindedness is pride.

God's character is such that He cannot lie, does not tolerate sin, knows everything (is omniscient), is everywhere (is omnipresent), and all-powerful (is omnipotent). Humans do not possess these qualities; thus, we are limited. Faith now steps in.

There are many, many hard truths about God. I have had to remove my own pride to accept Him. I don't know it all and, therefore, will never have all of the answers. Letting go of my ego became my first step in genuinely learning who God is and being open to understanding His ways.

Through my higher education at a liberal university, my professors often challenged me in my Christian beliefs. It wasn't always easy. Yet the more I was exposed to the complexity of the human body, animals, plants, and our world, it all pointed more and more to our intelligent and perfect God.

Many of you will choose to put this book down at this point because of your belief system. I simply ask you to continue to read this to the end with an open heart and mind. What can it hurt?

As Pascal wagered, what have you got to lose? Perhaps the only thing you might miss is the time you spent reading this book. More importantly, you might just gain everything. In the end, however, you might obtain an eternal relationship with something and someone bigger than yourself.

God created and wired us with a desire to know Him. If you are truly honest with yourself, deep down, you are searching for more. Your inner being longingly seeks to know and understand Him at a deeper level. Why not give Him an open door to your heart?

I'm excited for you to join me on this Theosynthesis journey. I believe this journey will impact your life at some level. I pray you will find new truths and a renewed connection to God.

CHAPTER 2

SCIENCE & GOD

AS A YOUNG FRESHMAN biology student at a liberal university in Texas, I was inundated from day one in zoology class regarding the theories of Darwin and evolution. Never once was anything ever mentioned about God. I mean, who would dare say God in this university setting of brilliant minds, right?

Unfortunately, this is the same case in our universities and schools. Darwin's theory of evolution is taught as fact. The public-school books mention nothing of the possibility of an intelligent designer. Therefore, students hear only one side of the argument.

It became evident to me that my professors very much believed in Darwin's theories, and any other schools of thought were not welcome in their classrooms. I had so many questions that went unanswered, and quite frankly, my questions were met with scowls and disdain. Had I not been the hardheaded young lady I was, I might have just kept my mouth shut and quietly accepted these teachings as fact.

Much to the grumblings of my professors, I did ask the tough questions. I am thankful I didn't stay quiet. As I continued challenging the topic of evolution, there was one question none of my professors were able to answer. This question was focused on how sex evolved.

Here was a typical banter:

"*You want me to believe that all living creatures evolved over millions of years, right? Over this long amount of time, individual animals and species began to evolve and become unique. How then did the act of sex evolve, and why? It certainly isn't the most efficient way for animals to procreate, right?*"

My point was to use logic and statistics in my line of questioning. If the Darwin Theory of Evolution were true, then sexual reproduction would have needed to evolve as well. For a species to perpetuate themselves, animals would have been asexual beings early in the evolutionary timeline. Asexual reproduction would have been the early form of procreation.[1] An animal can reproduce itself on its own, such as an amoeba that pinches off another part of itself to then create another amoeba.

My question, based on reason, asked at what point in time did an animal species form an entirely individual male and female version of itself? For sexual reproduction, this requires both a male and a female. Both of the animals would have had to develop (both fully male and fully female) at the *exact* time in history? If not, the species would not have continued to perpetuate.

By examining just *one* species of the animal kingdom, what then are the odds of a fully formed male and a fully developed female evolving simultaneously at the exact moment in time? Well, guess what? It takes many zeroes after 10 for this to work mathematically.

---

1   Lisa Lucidi, and Scott McDevitt for the Biology 1B, https://ucmp.berkeley.edu/glossary/gloss6/asexual.html, Accessed May 2020.

The logistical probability proves that this is not possible. Math itself demonstrates that this theory is not a viable thesis. Now try putting this theory in front of every single species of animal in the animal kingdom. Woah!

This was just one of my questions that were met with befuddlement and, quite frankly, anger. The clear message I received was to keep my mouth shut, and when they saw my hand go up, they looked the other way. It became clear; these professors were not willing to hear a different viewpoint. My questions indeed seemed to scare and anger them.

Science is known for its openness to new thoughts. However, when it comes to God, science closes the door. Doesn't this seem to fly in the face of what science claims itself to be? The *Houston Chronicle* had this quote[2]:

> "Science is not just the collection of data and facts about nature. Science involves a method of investigation of nature that allows the discovery of knowledge not previously known. A closed mind has no room for new knowledge. A closed mind is like a cup already full—you cannot add more liquid to the cup or new ideas to the mind. A closed mind cannot investigate or learn new things, as it has already decided the outcome. One of the first things a scientist learns is how to have an open mind."

Many scientists and doctors teach the belief that science and God collide, and the two disciplines cannot coexist together. This,

2   Brenner, Laurie, "Why Does a Scientist Need to Be Open-Minded?" Work - Chron.com, http://work.chron.com/scientist-need-openminded-9492.html, Accessed May 19, 2020.

The more I have studied living things, the more convinced beyond a shadow of a doubt a brilliant Creator named God orchestrated everything perfectly on this earth and throughout the universe.

my friends, is where I have found God to be evident in the most profound way. The more I have studied living things, the more convinced beyond a shadow of a doubt a brilliant Creator name God orchestrated everything perfectly on this earth and throughout the universe.

The study of cytology, cellular biology, or of living cells, points to simply amazing structures. With the discovery of the first cells, scientists initially believed them to be simple structures. The exploration of the microscope and cells challenged everything science knew of them up to that point.

Scientists still have much to learn about this complex matrix of DNA. The encoded information located in the center of every one of our trillions of cells is mind-blowing. Genetics, along with the study of DNA, is still a relatively new field with discoveries uncovered daily. It is exciting to examine all of the latest developments in this field of study.

Astonishingly, new studies have shown the mitochondrial DNA can be linked back to a single female.[3] Within our cells is an organelle or cell structure called the "mitochondria." The function of the mitochondria is for cellular energy, and within this structure, it contains its own unique DNA. Astonishing, scientific information, isn't it?

Back in 1987, mitochondrial DNA revealed that it only contains genetic material from the female and can, therefore, be

---

3   https://ghr.nlm.nih.gov/mitochondrial-dna, June 2018.

traced back in time. They coined the term "Mitochondrial Eve."[4] Interesting choice of names since many science researchers dismiss the God-connection in the scientific realm.

I believe God, in His wisdom, has given us exactly what we need to know and see to know He exists. Who knows what we will find as science continues to advance. The more science uncovers, the more I recognize the fingerprint pointing to an Almighty Creator.

Our DNA was created by God, and therefore, I know deep within our genetic blueprint is the information He placed within each one of us to seek Him out. Whether we accept to seek Him or not is our choice. He wisely created us to choose Him freely. God created man to be more than robots made to worship Him. That would be forced worship. No one desires forced love as it would then not be love.

I believe we are wired deep within our DNA to seek God, to know, and to trust Him. When we turn away from Him, we are turning away from the Almighty source of power, energy, knowledge, and love. I also believe that when humans turn from God, there is a void I call a "God-gap" within them, causing them to seek anything to fill this empty space. Inherently, they know something is missing, and yet they continue to fill this space with a variety of things and activities.

Without God in our lives, this God-gap is a void of Him. The cycle of Theosynthesis is not complete. When this happens, because God wired us to know Him, man will find themselves on a never-ending cycle of seeking satisfaction in their lives.

Ultimately, when we as humans turn from God, He allows us to live our lives the way we choose. A life apart from God leaves

---

4   Brandon Specktor-Senior Writer, https://www.livescience.com/mitochondrial-eve-first-human-homeland.html,October 28, 2019.

us with an empty hole. As we witness daily in our world right now, we have more instances of suicide, mental illness, disease, anger, and rage than ever before. I believe that as we move further away from God, we will continue to see these tragic situations escalating. Choosing life apart from God is wanting to say no to God's love.

Turning away from God leads us to the world we now live—a fallen world where man knows more than God, and the result is chaos, pain, and death. Thankfully, many millions of Christian believers do know God and seek Him daily.

Your beliefs regarding God are your own choice. You may choose to believe in Him or to deny Him. There is no middle ground on this one.

Science provides us with a glimpse into an amazing, intelligent God of the universe. The more science uncovers, the more these discoveries point to a designer who possesses thought and creativity. What an exciting time to be alive to witness the miracles of life that science continues to find!

CHAPTER 3

INTRODUCTION TO THEOSYNTHESIS

HAVING EXPLORED who God is and a little introduction about science, we can now dig into this concept of Theosynthesis. The way the word came to me was confirmation of what this term means. I'll explain this a bit more below. When we open ourselves up to being in tune with God and listening to Him, He gives us much more than we could ever imagine.

As I mentioned at the beginning of this book, I was at my computer preparing a wellness workshop. I became convicted as I tried to visualize how to marry the concepts of diet, exercise, and overall wellness or wholeness along with the God factor. For me, it has been abundantly apparent how you can be in the best physical condition, eat right, look great, and yet still not be whole.

By wholeness, I am referring to being in balance with your mind, your body, and within your spirit. All three are essential to being well and whole. These components are the essence of Theosynthesis.

We continually see examples of people who appear on the outside to have it all. Take a look at a popular magazine featuring Hollywood stars. Time and again, we read stories of those who seemed to be on top of the world. In reality, they were severely depressed, riddled with drug problems, and indeed not whole.

I am certainly not implying all of these examples involved people with no connection to God; however, it appears many are living their lives outside of God's realm. Maybe they were searching for Him yet never allowed Him into their lives. Perhaps they even denied Him. My point is, being beautiful, vibrant, talented, and fit will never, ever be enough if God is absent from your life.

Today, we are in the most information-rich era in our history. We have more information about eating correctly and being physically fit than ever before. Yet, obesity, disease, and mental illness are rampant in staggering statistics. Why is this?

While preparing my seminar, I continued to ponder this question of being whole in mind, body, and spirit. The word "Theosynthesis" came to my mind. I quickly scribbled it on a pad while continuing to work on my project. It then occurred to me to search the word on the Internet. I was sure it was out there, and I wanted to learn more about it.

Much to my surprise, nothing showed up? Really? Maybe I typed it wrong. Nope—nada—nothing! My mind was spinning as I realized God had just given me a new word! I clearly remember pushing my chair back and looking up and saying, "God, *did You just give me a new word?*" Now, what on Earth was I to do with this word?

I immediately bought the domain name and began the process of having "Theosynthesis" trademarked. I wasn't quite sure where all of this would lead; I just knew I was on to something important. I also recognized that God had entrusted me with this new task.

Let's break this word down to follow where I was going with my thought process:

"Theos" means God. Synthesis in the biological world is the combining of separate elements or substances to form a coherent whole. The Greek meaning of "syn" is together. A more natural way to define synthesis is to be in union with something.

In union with God! This was *exactly* the point I was trying to get across for my workshop. We can do all of the right things, such as healthy eating and exercising, yet without God in our lives—we are not whole. Something is missing, and when we try and fill it with anything other than God, we will eventually fall flat.

As I stared at the image of photosynthesis, the image of Theosynthesis came to life!

This simple diagram below provides a visual. Therefore, Theosynthesis is not a difficult concept. Things don't have to be super complicated, do they? Being in union with God is how He wired and created His people.

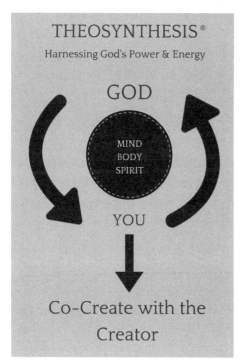

Many times in my own life, I have tried to make things more complicated than they needed to be. What I have found is more times than not, when I open my mind and stop trying to force my thoughts and opinions into them, things become clear. The keyword here is being *open*.

Just as in the cycle of photosynthesis where plants harness the sunlight's energy, we as God's chosen creation can harness the **Son** light. This happens by connecting with God in a variety of ways—prayer, meditation, worship, reading and studying His Word. Additionally, we can connect to God by simply being still and listening.

"Be still and know that I am God." Psalm 46:10 says just that. When we don't take time to be still before God, it becomes difficult to hear His voice. As I stated earlier, to know God, we must spend time getting to *know* Him. We will discuss the how and the why of getting to know God in the next few chapters.

The basics of Theosynthesis is to tune in to God. When a radio is not quite tuned in to the correct setting or station, it's difficult to hear the music or the information. When you turn the setting just a bit and connect with the perfect position on the dial, you can now enjoy your music or program.

The same principle occurs as we tune in and pay attention to Almighty God. The ability to tune in means being still enough for Him to tap into our minds and our hearts. For many of us, our hectic schedules, inability to disconnect from our cell phones, and social media keep us from hearing God. These lifestyle routines prevent us from connecting to our most important source—God.

When we discover we each have an incredible source to tap into through God, this can be life-changing. Freely accepting Him and giving our lives to His Son Jesus Christ, the power of the Holy Spirit enters into us. However, utilizing it is not always the case for many.

In the following chapters, we are going to discuss the how and the why of Theosynthesis. Let me leave you with a few essential

Scripture verses regarding the word "power." In the Bible, it now takes on an all-new meaning for me.

God created a perfect pattern to demonstrate to us His amazing provisions for man. He is the true source of all energy and light. When we truly recognize this and bow down before Him, He promises He is with all believers.

OLD TESTAMENT SCRIPTURES

*"This God is my **strong** refuge and has made my way blameless"* (2 Samuel 22:33).

*"Awesome is God from His sanctuary; the God of Israel—He is the One who gives **power** and strength to his people. Blessed be God." (Psalm 68:35).*

*"Your people will offer themselves freely on the day of Your **power**, in holy garments; from the womb of the morning, the dew of your youth will be yours" (Psalm 110:3).*

*"He gives **power** to the faint, and to Him who has no might He increases **strength**. Even youths shall faint and be weary, and young men shall fall exhausted; but they who wait for the LORD shall renew their **strength**; they shall mount up with wings like eagles; they shall run and not be weary; they shall walk and not faint" (Isaiah 40:29-31).*

*"Fear not, for I am with you; be not dismayed, for I am your God; I will **strengthen** you, I will help you, I will uphold you with my righteous right hand" (Isaiah 41:10).*

*"Ah, Lord GOD! It is you who have made the heavens and the earth by Your great **power** and by your outstretched arm! Nothing is too hard for you" (Jeremiah 32:17).*

NEW TESTAMENT SCRIPTURES

*"And then they will see the Son of Man coming in clouds with great **power** and glory" (Mark 13:26).*

*"And behold, I am sending the promise of my Father upon you. But stay in the city until you are clothed with **power** from on high" (Luke 24:49).*

*"But you will receive **power** when the Holy Spirit has come upon you, and you will be my witnesses in Jerusalem and in all Judea and Samaria, and to the end of the earth" (Acts 1:8).*

*"With great **power** the apostles continued to testify to the resurrection of the Lord Jesus. And God's grace was so powerfully at work in them all" (Acts 4:33).*

*"And Stephen, full of grace and **power**, was doing great wonders and signs among the people" (Acts 6:8).*

*"How God anointed Jesus of Nazareth with the Holy Spirit and with **power**" (Acts 10:38).*

"For I am not ashamed of the gospel, for it is the **power** of God for salvation to everyone who believes, to the Jew first and also to the Greek" (Romans 1:16).

"By the **power** of signs and wonders, by the **power** of the Spirit of God—so that from Jerusalem and all the way around to Illyricum I have fulfilled the ministry of the gospel of Christ" (Romans 15:19).

"For the word of the cross is folly to those who are perishing, but to us who are being saved it is the **power** of God" (1 Corinthians 1:18).

"But to those who are called, both Jews and Greeks, Christ the **power** of God and the wisdom of God" (1 Corinthians 1:24).

"That your faith might not rest in the wisdom of men but in the **power** of God" (1 Corinthians 2:5).

"When you are assembled in the name of the Lord Jesus and My spirit is present, with the **power** of our Lord Jesus" (1 Corinthians 5:4).

"And God raised the Lord and will also raise us up by His **power**" (1 Corinthians 6:14).

"By truthful speech, and the **power** of God; with the weapons of righteousness for the right hand and for the left" (2 Corinthians 6:7).

"But He said to me, 'My grace is sufficient for you, for My **power** is made perfect in weakness.' Therefore I will boast all the more gladly of my weaknesses, so that the **power** of Christ may rest upon me" (2 Corinthians 12:9).

"For He was crucified in weakness, but lives by the **power** of God. For we also are weak in Him, but in dealing with you we will live with Him by the **power** of God" (2 Corinthians 13:4).

"And what is the immeasurable greatness of His **power** toward us who believe, according to the working of his great might" (Ephesians 1:19).

"That according to the riches of His glory He may grant you to be **strengthened** with **power** through His Spirit in your inner being." (Ephesians 3:16).

"Now to Him who is able to do far more abundantly than all that we ask or think, according to the **power** at work within us" (Ephesians 3:20).

"Finally, be strong in the Lord and in the **strength** of His **might**" (Ephesians 6:10).

"Who will transform our lowly body to be like His glorious body, by the **power** that enables Him even to subject all things to Himself" (Philippians 3:21).

"*I can do all things through Him who **strengthens** me.*" (*Philippians 4:13*).

"*May you be **strengthened** with all **power**, according to his glorious might, for all endurance and patience with joy*" (*Colossians 1:11*).

"*Having been buried with him in baptism, in which you were also raised with him through faith in the **powerful** working of God, who raised him from the dead*" (*Colossians 2:12*).

"*Because our gospel came to you not only in word, but also in **power** and in the Holy Spirit and with full conviction*" (*1 Thessalonians 1:5*).

"*They will suffer the punishment of eternal destruction, away from the presence of the Lord and from the glory of His **might***" (*2 Thessalonians 1:9*).

"*Therefore do not be ashamed of the testimony about our Lord, nor of me his prisoner, but share in suffering for the gospel by the **power** of God*" (*2 Timothy 1:8*).

"*He is the radiance of the glory of God and the exact imprint of His nature, and He upholds the universe by the word of His **power***" (*Hebrews 1:3*).

"*And have tasted the goodness of the word of God and the **powers** of the age to come*" (*Hebrews 6:5*).

*"Who by God's **power** are being guarded through faith for a salvation ready to be revealed in the last time" (1 Peter 1:5).*

*"Who has gone into heaven and is at the right hand of God, with angels, authorities, and **powers** having been subjected to him" (1 Peter 3:22).*

*"For we did not follow cleverly devised myths when we made known to you the **power** and coming of our Lord Jesus Christ, but we were eyewitnesses of His majesty" (2 Peter 1:16).*

*"We give thanks to you, Lord God Almighty, who is and who was, for you have taken your great **power** and begun to reign" (Revelation 11:17).*

CHAPTER 4

THE "HOW" OF THEOSYNTHESIS

ISN'T GOD'S WORD amazing? Interwoven in Scripture, the Words remind us of His mighty power. Straight from God, they confirm over and over that as believers, we too have the rich power of the Holy Spirit. Imagine—the power of the Spirit dwelt within each of us—this is a game-changer.

BELIEF AND FAITH

God promised His love, acceptance, and power to all who humbly seek Him. Therefore, the very first step in tapping into His power source is by understanding what it means to have belief and faith in Him. Many of us are familiar with John 3:16:

> *"For God so loved the world that He gave His only begotten Son. That whomsoever believes in Him shall not perish but have everlasting life."*

God **SO** loved the world. Love is the central theme throughout this entire verse. Love, therefore, holds the greatest of power, doesn't it? We hear people saying all of the time how love conquers all, and love will change the world. They are correct, yet knowing where the real source of love comes from is vital.

Next, we see the statement, "He **GAVE**." When you freely give something to someone, we call this a "gift." Jesus was God's free gift to humanity. He gave us Jesus freely and out of love. Not a difficult concept, but unfortunately, it's one that causes many to disregard and reject Jesus.

"His **ONLY** begotten Son." Jesus is the only created Being from God who was sent to us as a sinless sacrifice to atone for our sins. There are no others who can claim this.

"Whomsoever **BELIEVES** in Him." Yes, anyone who sincerely accepts Christ as their Savior becomes saved from their sins. There is no secret here; the concept is not hard. Accepting Christ to spend eternity with God and to tap into His power source is a promise. Humanity just has to put down his or her agenda and bow to the Almighty.

"Shall not perish but have everlasting **LIFE**." When we fully accept and believe in Jesus, He promises we will only die once. Our physical bodies will die a physical death, yet we as Christians have also been promised eternal life with Him.

Although this Scripture is inspirational, the part about God giving His only Son is difficult to accept by most. Many people just cannot allow themselves to believe that God would do such a selfless act for them.

Perhaps they feel they have done too many bad things in their lives to think a loving God would do this for them. They simply don't feel worthy.

He did, however! And He did it for every person on this earth. How His heart must break when He knows there will be those who refuse to ever accept His wonderful gift. Have you ever experience having a gift that was rejected? Have you ever been rejected by others? Neither of these types of rejection is a good thing. It is painful.

CONNECTING WITH GOD

Once a person chooses to accept Jesus as their Lord and Savior, it is essential to then connect with Him. Just as an electrical appliance will not work without plugging it into a power source, we as Christians are to be plugged into our power source—God. Again, this is where many short-circuit the message.

Accepting Christ into your life is the first step. Learning to connect with the Almighty is the next step. This latter action is more difficult as it requires dedication, study, prayer, resilience, discipline, and the desire to make some changes in your life.

As humans, we like running our own lives. We resist having someone or something dictating to us. God understands this and, therefore, does not force Himself on us. He patiently waits for us to seek Him.

One of the most critical steps after accepting Christ is to connect with Him eagerly. There are so many ways to do this. The most crucial step is to know God's Word.

The Bible to many can be quite daunting as a foreign book they fear they cannot understand. God promises that if we seek Him, He will find us. He is there to gently guide us along our path of trying to know Him. Let's take a look at a few scriptures on this:

"But seek first the kingdom of God and His righteousness, and all these things will be added to you" (Matthew 6:33).

"Do not be conformed to this world, but be transformed by the renewal of your mind, that by testing you may discern what is the will of God, what is good and acceptable and perfect" (Romans 12:2).

Right away in Matthew, it is clear we must seek God *first* in all that we do. Following in Romans, we see the writings of Paul who wisely counsels how the renewing of our minds must transform us. This renewal comes from spending time knowing God and knowing His Word.

When we study any subject, we gain new knowledge about the topic. When we approach God's Word with an open heart and mind, He will show us what we need. His Word is living and was supremely and flawlessly written as our guidebook to know Him and to understand His character.

Prayer and meditation are ways we use to connect with God. The word "meditation" has taken on a negative meaning for many Christians. Many people associate meditation with eastern religious teachings and secular teachings and thereby fear it is something with which they should not associate.

When we are still and simply focus on God and remain quiet to listen to His voice, we can experience the power of meditation. There are scientific studies that actually prove the human brain during meditation reaps many, many benefits.[1] Meditation is a way to connect with God quietly and powerfully.

Some of the most highly regarded universities and medical schools have published studies regarding the effects of meditation

---

1   https://www.nccih.nih.gov/health/meditation-in-depth.

on the human brain. Yale University and Johns Hopkins University both have very fascinating studies regarding this topic.[2]

A few of the benefits of meditation they have researched include:

- improvement with areas of concentration and attention
- alleviation and reduction of social anxiety and anxiety in general
- improvement in the mood centers of the brain as a result of cellular changes within the brain found in the area of the amygdala
- higher resistance of the gray matter within the brain as it ages[3]
- excellent results in the areas of treating addiction

Prayer is a form of meditation. Since God created us, wouldn't it make sense that He wired our brains to benefit from spending time with Him? Seeing the scientific proof of this is exciting, yet our ancestors inherently knew the benefits of spending time in prayer and reflection. Why then is this so difficult for humans today?

I can say in my own life when I stray from spending time with God, I sense I have missed out on my connection source. If I continue racing ahead without including Him, life can spiral out of control very quickly. I don't handle stress as well, nor do I respond well to those around me when I lose my God-connection.

Life in the 21st Century has become hectic for most people. Upon awakening, we immediately connect to our cell phones, fill our minds with the radio or TV, run here and there with all sorts

---

2   https://www.hopkinsmedicine.org/health/wellness-and-prevention/need-stress-relief-try-mindfulness-meditation; https://news.yale.edu/2011/11/21/tuning-out-how-brains-benefit-meditation.

3   Alice G. Walton, "7 Ways Meditation Can Actually Change the Brain," 2018.

of activities, and rarely just stop to pray or meditate. The results are stressed-out, anxiety-riddled, and unhappy people.

Taking time to be alone with God by reading His Word, talking to Him, or just sitting quietly with Him can change your life immensely.

Taking time to be alone with God by reading His Word, talking to Him, or just sitting quietly with Him can change your life immensely. Discipline and personal priorities become essential to bring God into the forefront of your life. One must make time for God and prioritize Him into your daily routine.

Take a look at all of the things we do have time for in a typical day. Time spent on the phone, eating, getting dressed, watching a favorite TV show, driving our cars, running errands, exercising, hobbies, and work. These are just a few activities that fill our day. The most crucial activity, however, is slowing down to spend time with God.

I have found that when I stop and focus on God, I relax, let go, and feel completely renewed. Spending time alone with God can energize you and give you the boost you need. Learning to slow down for God requires putting it as the number-one priority every day.

Most likely, if you evaluated any given day on your calendar, you could identify something you could give up to carve out time to spend with God. Again, this is a choice each one of us must make. Choosing to tap into the Almighty Power Source for me has dramatically changed and impacted my life.

There are many other ways to connect with God as well. Spending time in worship is a necessary act. Singing to Him, worshipping together with other believers, and even taking the time to recognize His amazing creation are ways to connect with Him. Something as simple as turning off the radio on a long commute to work is an excellent way to spend time in quiet reflection and prayer.

Isn't it a beautiful how God designed a way for us to tap into Him directly? This power is a gift to us all. I hope you will begin to discover this energy source you have in God, which is available to you this very moment.

What do you need to let go of to give God the time He deserves? How might your life look completely different if you gave Him just a few minutes a day? I bet once you recognize the peace you feel, you will desire to spend more and more time with Him.

CHAPTER 5

THE WHY OF THEOSYNTHESIS

WE HAVE WALKED through the "how" of tapping into God's power; therefore, why we should do this seems like it would be a no-brainer. Unfortunately, many will scoff at this entire thought process and continue down their path, desperately seeking their source of power. Eventually, however, their self-directed power source will fizzle out. Desperately trying to do life on our own will ultimately prove we cannot handle it all within our power.

In our world today, we have become a society of me, me, me, if-it's-to-be-it's-up-to-me mentality. Our TV shows have become extremely narcissistic with the focus being on getting what you want no matter which person you must step on to get it.

Many people today believe they can make up their own rules, change laws if they don't agree with them, and live without a moral compass. We also see those opposing the Ten Commandments of the Bible. These people are screaming to have them removed from our courtrooms and schools.

During my lifetime, I have watched prayer being removed from our schools and athletic events. The definition of marriage is now being revised by our court system. Society is slowly weaving in a new interpretation for the definition of what it means to be a male or female. Morality itself is being redefined as our world continues to change rapidly.

Historically, civilizations that allow the moral decay of its society will eventually crumble. There is a reason for moral laws, and without these fundamental truths, the culture and its people lose their way. The result is destruction.

Regardless of what people say they want, there must be moral laws to guide any society. Whether people want to believe it or not, the founding fathers of the United States of America were guided by Christian ethical principles. Freedom of religion is teetering on a tightrope right now. We see for the first time in the United States freedom *from* religion forced on us.

Story after story on the news reminds us of religious persecution happening all over the world. Alarmingly, this persecution has infiltrated our nation at a stealthy pace. The more the courts, schools, and businesses continue to remove any mention of God, the more depraved and immoral our country has come become.

As Christians today, we seem to be the one group many feel they can tear down and openly criticize. We do just about anything to protect other religions so that we won't offend them, yet no one seems to be bothered when Christians are being ridiculed and persecuted. This behavior is happening daily, and it is getting worse.

The why of Theosynthesis is simply God calling us to tap into His power source. His power is our only defense against what is happening today. More now than ever, Christians need to be in prayer, studying God's Word, and preparing for a world that is quickly becoming more hostile to our faith and beliefs.

More, now than ever, Christians need to be in prayer, studying God's Word and preparing for a world that is quickly becoming more hostile to our faith and beliefs.

There are many examples throughout the Bible of God calling His people to turn to Him. In the days of Moses, God continued to guide His people to Him. From the destruction of Sodom and Gomorrah to the worldwide flood, God continues to warn His people of the coming destruction.

Today as we watch the moral fabric of society becoming tattered and frayed, it is more important than ever for Christians to take a stand for God. We must stay connected to Him and one another. We must arm ourselves with the power of the Holy Spirit to fight the good fight.

It is easy to grow weary of the onslaught of what we are currently seeing in our society. Powering up and teaming up with God will aid us in remaining strong and keeping us on the right path. He never promised us it would be easy, but He does guarantee He is with us always.

As we close this chapter, I hope you see the importance of the "why." Now is the time, friends, to connect with God earnestly and urgently. Using the example of photosynthesis, plants harness the power of the sunlight during the day while in the cover of darkness at night, they continue working. To be prepared for the harvest, these plants work both day and night.

Are you preparing your life to reap the abundance of God? Are you growing your roots deeply into the spiritual soil of Christ? Finally, are you planting today to reap God's harvest in your life?

THEOSYNTHESIS®

PART II
UNIVERSAL TRUTHS OF GOD

CHAPTER 6

KNOWING GOD'S WILL

AS A CHRISTIAN, I hear the saying, "If it's God's will…" Many people don't comprehend what this statement means, while others find it to be a convenient way to quickly put something off on God. Let's take a closer look at the meaning and intention of using the words "God's will."

To know God's will, we must first take a look at the character and the makeup of God. As we know, God is omnipresent meaning He is in all things. He is omnipotent, meaning all-powerful, and is omniscient, meaning knowing all things. The prefix "omni" simply means "all." Therefore, the God we know is always around us. He is all-powerful, all-knowing, and understanding.

The fantastic design of the human brain allows it to think in time and dimension. It's difficult to wrap our minds around something that doesn't fit into those confines. Therefore, this concept is a tough to understand, and this is where faith comes in. Accepting that we cannot and will not know or even understand everything can be frustrating. Nevertheless, this is a crucial hurdle for many to overcome.

In Revelation 1:8, we see how perfectly this concept reads:

"'I AM the Alpha and the Omega,' says the Lord God, 'who is and who was, and who is to come, the Almighty.'"

He is the Alpha, which is the beginning, and the Omega, which is the end, who IS, WAS, and IS TO COME. It's apparent in this verse to see our Almighty God as an omnipresent being. Omnipresent means that God is ever-present and with us always.

We simply cannot put God in a box. Our finite minds will never be able to grasp the concept of who He really and fully is. If we are to put our trust and beliefs in the Almighty God, we must accept Him as being an omnipresent being.

Charles H. Spurgeon, the 19th-century theologian, explains it this way[1]:

"We believe that he [God] filleth heaven and earth, and hell; that he is in the very space which his creation seems to claim, for creatures do not displease God; and even space which is occupied by his handiworks is still filled with himself. The rocky bowels of the unsearched-out depths are full of God; where the sea roars, or where the solid granite leaves no interstice or vacuum, even there is God; not only in the open place, and in the chasm, but penetrating all matter, and abounding everywhere in all, and filling all things with himself."

Omniscient (knows all) and omnipotent (can do anything); therefore, He does have a will, a mind, and a presence in this world. To know anyone's mind or their will and desires, we must first

---

1   Charles H. Spurgeon, https://www.allaboutgod.com/omnipresence-definition-faq.htm.

identify with them on some level. Therefore, we must seek to know God if we are to understand His will.

Therefore, an omnipresent God is always with us. The Hebrew word Emmanuel means God with us. We see this in Matthew 1:23:

> *"The virgin will be with child and will give birth to a son, and they will call Him Emmanuel, which means God with us."*

How then do we come to know God? As we have outlined and discussed in previous chapters, accepting Him, spending time with Him, and studying His Word are critically important steps in knowing Him and understanding His will for our lives. So many people miss this point. They continue to ask God for things or to blame Him when things don't go as they would like, yet they never invest in getting to know Him.

An omnipotent God is all-powerful, which is often thought of negatively. People envision God upon His throne, simply playing chess with His people on Earth. Rather than thinking of God with an iron fist, imagine Him in terms of His power being unlimited. As we have discussed in the earlier chapters about God's character, He cannot go against His nature.

Evil is not in His nature; therefore, He will not engage in evil things. He cannot contradict His character. He will not lie, nor will He condone sin. These are simply not in His nature.

> *"Great is our Lord and mighty in power, His understanding has no limit"* (Psalm 147:5).

Let's take a look at the final omni word, omniscient. Sometimes, I have said, "Wouldn't it be great to be able to know all things?" On second thought, having the complete ability to understand all things would be a huge responsibility. You would know when events were going to happen. You would know the true motives of other people, and you would also see the date when you will die. The same would be true for those you love.

After pondering this thought, I am glad I can't be all-knowing. Almighty God does know all things. Therefore, imagine how His heart must bear the knowledge and pain of the depths of human sin. How He must anguish over the poor decisions we all make that have lasting effects on our own lives and on others.

> *"Who can fathom the Spirit of the LORD, or instruct the LORD as his counselor? Whom did the LORD consult to enlighten him, and who taught him the right way? Who was it that taught him knowledge, or showed him the path of understanding?" (Isaiah 40:13–14).*

Having now discussed God's character of being all-knowing, all-powerful, and in all things, how can we know His will for our lives? Once we become Christians, we begin our quest to understand what it is God desperately wants from us.

As I have pondered this question, I created an acrostic as a guide for how to know God's will in your life. If you can remember the word FOLLOW as your guide, learning to seek Him daily will be much easier.

F.O.L.L.O.W.

FOLLOW HIM

Read, study, and know His Word. It's difficult to follow someone when you don't know what they stand for. By soaking in God's Word, this is a great way to begin understanding His will in your life.

> *"Again Jesus spoke to them, saying, 'I am the light of the world. Whoever follows me will not walk in darkness, but will have the light of life'" (John 8:12).*

> *"'Whoever does not take up their cross and follow me is not worthy of me'" (Matthew 10:38).*

> *"To this you were called, because Christ suffered for you, leaving you an example, that you should follow in his steps" (1 Peter 2:21).*

OBEY HIS LAWS

God gives us a very detailed and descriptive narrative in the Bible regarding what He allows and what He does not allow. You will never achieve perfection as only Jesus did, but striving diligently and daily to obey His commands will help you in knowing God's will for your life. Only in obedience can we move from our sinful lives and begin moving day by day into the path He desires for us.

God's wish for each of us is to live fully each and every day.

God's wish for each of us is to live fully every day. When we obey His commands, we can then set our paths on a righteous path. Obedience is a necessary step in knowing God's will. Righteousness is acting by following the divine or moral law, morally right or justifiable.

> "*Love the Lord your God and keep His requirements, His decrees, His laws, and His commands always*" (Deuteronomy 11:1).

> "'*If you love Me, keep My commands*'" (John 14:15).

> "*But whoever looks intently into the perfect law that gives freedom, and continues in it—not forgetting what they have heard, but doing it—they will be blessed in what they do.*" (James 1:25).

Do you see that where the verse in James says, "…looks intently into the perfect law that gives freedom…"? Casually flipping the Bible open is not what God wants. He desires you to look intently at the Scriptures. He wants us to study the Bible to know it.

His laws give you freedom from the sin that once condemned you to hell. It now has no hold over you. Yes, you will still fail to live a perfect life. Rest in knowing through a perfect Savior, the sin that once held you in bondage is no more. You are free from the condemnation of sin.

LOVE HIM

To follow anything or anyone with a pure heart requires love. Love is the fuel and the passion for going after something, fighting for, and dying for it if necessary.

> "*For God so loved the world that He gave His only begotten Son, that whosoever should believe in Him shall never perish*" (John 3:16).

God has shown His immense love for us through the sacrifice of Jesus. If you sincerely wish to know His will, accepting and loving His Son Jesus as your personal Savior is crucial. Dedicating the time to study His word and understanding His character, will undoubtedly help you gain a much clearer vision of His will for your life.

LEAVE YOUR FORMER LIFE

When you decide to follow Christ, there must be some evidence of leaving your sinful, previous ways behind. Often, we witness this in another person's life when a radical change occurs after they give their hearts and lives to Christ. Another person may see more gradual changes over time. Either way, leaving old sinful habits is a continuous sanctification process that is needed to follow Christ.

Sanctification is the state of growing in divine grace as a result of Christian commitment after baptism or conversion.

> "*You were taught, with regard to your former way of life, to put off your old self, which is being corrupted by its deceitful desires;*" (Ephesians 4:22).

We cannot merely repent of our old ways, and we must be continually transformed into a new creation if we are to follow Him. We must be convicted within our spirit and can no longer be content in continuing to live in sinful ways. Seeking God by sincerely repenting and turning to a new way of living is an essential key in knowing God.

OFFER YOUR TALENTS

Another crucial aspect of knowing God's will in your life is discovering your God-given talents. Once identified, you must begin utilizing them in a way that will please God. He says in His word that we all have gifts and talents. We will discuss this topic in greater detail in Chapter 18.

Bottom line, everyone has something they can use for God's kingdom. No matter how small or how large, God has gifted you with some skill or talent in which you can further His work. Your job is to ask Him to help you discover these gifts and talents and then to begin using them.

> "For we are God's handiwork, created in Christ Jesus to do good works, which God prepared in advance for us to do" (Ephesians 2:10).

> "Each of you should use whatever gift you have received to serve others, as faithful stewards of God's grace in its various forms" (1 Peter 4:10).

WORTHINESS

The Merriam-Webster Dictionary defines worthy as being good enough, deserving attention, or respect. In this instance, we are referring to being righteous before God. What does this mean exactly?

When you were a small child, more than likely, it was necessary to please your parents. To do so, you followed their rules. With God, He sees all of His children as worthy. Even when we fail, He still loves us and cares for us.

Therefore, as a believer, you are worthy. Allow this truth to soak in for a moment. Nothing you can do on your own earns you this title. God, who is almighty, loves each one of us and sees us as worthy.

The main message is this: Getting to know God is the only way to know and understand His will for your life. If you are sincere in wanting to know Almighty God, remember and apply the FOLLOW pattern, and you will be one step closer to discovering His will and purpose for your life.

CHAPTER 7

CONNECTING WITH GOD

IN WRITING this chapter, I thought a lot about the word "connection." When we meet someone, we experience some relationship with them. It may be a positive exchange, or it could be a negative encounter. A connection then is simply a link you have with someone or something. In this chapter, as we discuss the concept of connecting to God, I believe you too will understand the importance of why this topic.

To know God's will for our lives, we must connect to Him. When God created man, He knew it was not good for man to be alone. He designed us to need connected relationships with other people.

He also knew we need a connection with Him. He deeply desires to have a strong relationship with every one of us. His ultimate desire is for His people to turn to Him through an intentional connection. God didn't just create us as trophies to place on His heavenly shelf.

Recently, I was in an antique shop in Waco, Texas, and struck up a conversation with the owner of the business. I inquired about the beautiful antique crosses, which naturally kicked off a discussion about God. It seemed quite natural to ask him about his belief in God as he apparently had a sincere fascination in finding and studying these old relic crosses.

He began sharing the story of when he was about eight years old, that he almost died from a horrific illness. When he was the sickest during this time, he would have vivid dreams of what he described as a rope that connected himself to God. He knew even at the age of eight that this rope represented a lifeline to God.

He continued his story, sharing during the course of his life, and this dream has never left him. The only changing part in the dream occurs when he either pulls away from God or turns toward Him. During the times of rebellion, he explained, the rope would become frayed and weakened. When he was attending church, in prayer, and living the life he should, the dreams would be that of a healthy and intact cord.

As I listened to this beautiful and visual story, it made sense to me that these cords are perhaps truly there for all of us. Imagine for a moment that each of us have an invisible cord that's a direct connection to God! I like this visual, and it gives me great hope.

Another cord concept is the one within a mother's womb. The umbilical cord is the direct connection to gain sustenance for growth and to obtain nutrients. Once born, this umbilical cord is severed.

What if, however, God provides all of us with His umbilical cord that's never severed unless we choose to let go of it? It is there, and it's durable and supportive when we maintain our relationship with God. However, when we decide to turn from Him, this precious lifeline weakens.

Just as an umbilical cord provides the necessary nutrients for a growing fetus, God's umbilical cord provides believers the required spiritual nutrients as we grow in Christ. I love this analogy, and it helps me comprehend why we must stay connected to God.

As I began researching the anatomy of the umbilical cord, it was interesting to note the fantastic design of this structure. The structure is tube-like, which functions as a two-way street between the developing fetus and the mother.

Nutrients from the mother are shared with the baby via the umbilical cord. Subsequently, waste products from the developing baby transfer to the mother. Upon a closer study of the anatomy of the umbilical cord, it has the shape of a spiral, very much in line with the double helix design we see in our DNA.

Additionally, there are three primary cords or veins within the umbilicus. The entire umbilical cord is durable. Surrounding the conduits within the umbilicus is a cellular substance named Wharton's Jelly that was introduced by Dr. Thomas Wharton in 1656.[1]

This jelly serves in preventing the cords within the main structure of the umbilicus from becoming kinked while in utero. It was called jelly because of its mucosal characteristics, which aids in cushioning the three vessels within the umbilical cord. Because of this design, the cord can protect the all-important nutrient/waste exchange.

How cool is that? If we imagine an invisible umbilical cord connected to God, visualize this cord delivering to us the goodness from

1   John E. Davis, Armand Keating, John T. Walker, https://stcmcellsjournals. onlinelibrary.wiley.com/doi/full/10.1002/sctm.16-0492, May 10, 2017.

If we imagine an invisible umbilical cord connected to God, visualize this cord delivering to us the goodness from Him, while relinquishing the toxins in our lives. As we pour into Him, we are able to give God those things which are no longer serving us.

Him, while relinquishing the toxins in our lives. As we pour into Him, we can give God those things that are no longer serving us.

I love this about God! His exact and precise design of every inch of our bodies points to His perfect design. He is the Master Designer.

Now, correlate this to the verse from Ecclesiastes.

"Though one may be overpowered, two can defend themselves. A cord of three strands is not quickly broken" (Ecclesiastes 4:12).

The perfect structure of the umbilical cord is three strands. How fantastic is that? The mind is blown!

He designed us to be and to stay connected to Him. Theosynthesis then is just that. The connection to God that He created perfectly for us. When we choose to turn away from God, this precious cord is frayed and can ultimately break. Because we are designed to know God, therein lies the problem. If we choose to live our lives independent of God, this lifeline is absent, thereby leaving us on our own.

Without a secure connection to God, we indeed are on our own. Has being on your own, absent of God, worked for you? If not, what do you need to do today to begin to repair this all-important God-cord connection to Him?

CHAPTER 8

CONNECTING TO OTHERS

AS WE CONTINUE this discussion regarding connections, now we can explore the importance of connecting to others. Way back in the Book of Genesis, we read where God created man and saw He needed a helpmate. In His ultimate wisdom, God recognized how He designed us, and it would be necessary for having connected relationships with other humans.

As we know, healthy relationships in our lives enrich us deeply. New studies of infants abandoned at birth and who received very little human interaction clearly shows that these infants experienced stunted physical growth. Babies who have not received direct contact with a loving human did not thrive as those of the babies who were cared for in a nurturing environment.

Going back to the umbilical cord illustration in the last chapter, when a baby is born and the umbilical cord cut, the child must now genuinely depend on someone for its food source and care to survive. The child must also receive a strong human bond if he or she is to grow and thrive fully.

The human connection is strong. While observing young children playing in a park with other children, you can quickly see how they are naturally drawn to the other children. They gravitate toward one another to connect and to play. They do this usually if left on their own.

What happens as we experience connections in life? Many times, bonds break when relationships fail. Trust breaks, hearts are wounded, and often, we are hurt the most by the action or words of others. When emotional pain is involved, we often retreat from others. We have been broken by other humans so much, and we desire to withdraw and to be alone.

Sadly, this is the result of the sin cycle in our world. We as believers are the people God has chosen to maintain connections with others. We are to be the people who continue to reach the unreachable, love the unlovable, and repair broken relationships when at all possible.

In our discussion of Theosynthesis, connecting is critical. God's entire design of His people depends on them helping one another, serving one and uplifting another. In Matthew 4:4, "*Man cannot live by bread alone*," has a much deeper meaning than to discuss the nutritional needs of our body.

God created His people to be much more complex biological beings than to ingest and digest food. We are incredibly complex beings from the inner-workings of our cellular makeup to the unexplainable emotions of the human brain. I am genuinely excited about the discussion of macroevolution.

MACROEVOLUTION

Stay with me for a moment as we look into this topic. Macroevolution refers to massive changes over time, such as one species of an animal changing into another completely different type of animal. Take a look at the absence of an example of an amphibious water animal morphing into a reptile-like land creature over time.

In contrast, microevolution refers to small changes over time within its species. The beak of a bird adapting to its environment to properly pull worms out of the earth, as Darwin observed, is an example of a microevolutionary change. These types of changes do not cause a kind of species to morph into another.

The keyword in studying macroevolution is the term, "observed." The problem with macroevolution is that it's not possible to observe this process. If this process takes millions and millions of years, there is no possible way for it to be seen.

Additionally, the existence of any fossil evidence of these transitional animals does not exist. Those who perpetuate Darwin's Theory of Evolution seem to gloss over this significant fact. Therefore, his theory remains just that, a theory, not a law.

As science continues to discover more about the human brain and emotions, the study of psychology and the in-depth of complex human behavior continues to boggle the minds of the medical community. There is no simple explanation for the range of human emotion. Sure, we can study the various hormonal chemicals flowing through our bodies which affect feeling, yet there is no scientific explanation for all of the varying degrees of human emotion.

What causes one person to burst into tears, while another is unaffected? In scientific terms, this phenomenon cannot be explained scientifically. Human emotion is exceptionally complex. Human behavior is even more of a mystery.

What we do know is the fact that humans thrive more efficiently when they are connecting with other humans. Isolation from man is used very effectively in prisons and with those who are being tortured or punished. Time and again, these isolated individuals suffer severe and lasting psychological damage.

My point is, we are wired to have relationships with other human beings. Down in our deepest levels, we desire to have friends and family we can connect with regularly. God intended for us to live in harmony and work together with our fellow man.

When sin entered the world, man became faced with choices. Either we follow God's guidelines, or we choose to disobey them. As we have discussed earlier, God created us with the option of free will. When people choose to sin, it ultimately affects others. Those who want to follow Christ must be the conduits in helping maintain healthy interpersonal connections.

I love the verse from Proverbs 17:17 that says, "*A friend loves at all times, and a brother is born for a time of adversity.*" This verse sums up perfectly the importance of human interaction. Love, of course, is the root of human connection. Devoid of love and without any moral standards, this world would become completely dark and evil.

No matter how complicated relationships can be, take to heart as believers that we must maintain meaningful connections to others and the world. We are required to model Christ's love through us and with other people. When we are living the lives we are commanded as Christians, His light will shine through us. Others will see it and hopefully desire to seek God's light as a result.

I'm certainly not suggesting by merely working on keeping relationships healthy, they will be. In fact, as a Christian, your light will often be the very thing that repulses a non-Christian. Your light illuminates the darkness, including those with dark hearts.

I have experienced this many times. For no reason at all, someone does not choose to be around you. Take heart, though, and never allow your light for Christ to dim. Even when your light is rejected, you are still a beacon of hope in this fallen world.

In this day and age of modern technology supposedly designed to keep us connected, studies are showing it is having the opposite effect on people. Have you noticed people are communicating face-to-face less and less with the advent of text messaging, emails, and social media?

This amazing technology was supposed to assist us in staying connected in a much more efficient way. While we can quickly transfer instant information to one another, we are discovering that we are losing our ability to communicate in person. As a mother of grown children, I can attest to this as a very true statement.

I often say to my children, "Just call me!" I cannot hear their voice, their tone, or their emotions from a text message. As we lose touch with one another through authentic face-to-face connections, I fear the result will be detrimental to humans. God designed humans for interpersonal interactions.

While these technological advances are handy, they will never replace a real human connection, and I hope they never will. Be aware as you communicate and connect with your friends and family. Please encourage them to come together personally when they can. There is simply no replacement for in-person interactions.

Blessings to you as you navigate your on-Earth relationships. No doubt, relationships will be challenging, yet we are genuinely called to maintain these connections. As Christians, we are to be a joyful connection to those around us!

CHAPTER 9

CONNECTING TO SELF

ARE YOU CONNECTING to self? While this thought may seem counterintuitive at first glance, this is an area many people gloss over. Of course, we know ourselves better than anyone else; therefore, connecting to yourself may seem a bit odd. Why on earth would we need to connect to ourselves?

While working on this book with diligent research, I am convinced more than ever of the importance of connecting to oneself. What I mean by connecting to self is this—knowing and understanding our true selves on a deep and transparent level. Being authentic and honest with ourselves allows us the ability to be able to serve others in this world.

To truly connect with and within the lives of others, we must first be able to plug into our most in-depth and innermost thoughts. What makes you and I tick? What makes us laugh, cry, become angry, or causes us to love or creates stress?

Bookstores and blog sites contain hundreds of self-help books regarding loving and accepting yourself. The points in these narratives are valid, yet many of them are missing the main ingredient—God. Without God, there is a gap. Those who choose to follow God and obey His Word present themselves with a deep and abiding peace that defies understanding.

Ephesians 2:10 says, "*For we are his workmanship, created in Christ Jesus for good works, which God prepared beforehand, that we should walk in them.*" When we fully grasp what this verse means, accepting who you are, created by God, is a huge step in being able to then connect to your inner spirit.

Do you see this? The verse above says, "*His workmanship, created in Christ for good works which He prepared beforehand!*" You are not an accident or a mistake. No matter what the circumstances surrounding your conception, you were planned before you were ever born.

If you struggle with this concept, go back and reread this verse. Knowing a loving Creator designed every inch of you should help put any self-doubts, self-hating, self-loathing thoughts to rest. A healthy self-connection, therefore, is not about being boastful or full of yourself; it truly means being content within your spirit.

The longer I am here on this earth, the more I fully understand what it means to connect to self. In my younger years, it seemed I needed to be going 100 percent, 24 hours a day. Keeping a packed schedule is one way to ensure you will never have the quiet time you need to reflect and focus on your inner self.

After my first major health setback, I found myself with a ton of time in which to think and reflect. I was 43 years old and given the dreaded news of a massive tumor the size of an orange in my right chest. I remember the doctor calling me and saying, "Your chest X-ray shows a large mass. You need to get to the Houston medical center stat!"

My mind went numb. No one can predict how you will react to hearing this type of news. I am sure many of you reading this can relate. For me, it felt like I was in a dream moving in slow motion.

After visiting with a top thoracic surgeon in Houston, he looked at me squarely in the face and said, "Darlin, I've got to operate on ya!" Just like that, in his warm Texan drawl, he let me know I was not going home that day.

The next few days were a complete blur as I underwent test after test. I was poked, prodded, scanned, and examined more times than I could count. The team of physicians were trying to figure out what type of tumor was deep inside my chest.

Finally, on the third night in the hospital, a team of doctors showed up in my room looking quite grave. The consensus was a tumor of the thymus gland, thus suggesting possible non-Hodgkin's lymphoma. It didn't look good at all. They suggested I get my affairs in order, sign a living will, and other directives in the event I didn't survive the operation.

The night before the surgery, I was all alone in my hospital room and planned my funeral. It was strange to think about it. I also spent the entire night writing letters to the important people in my life.

The reason I share this story here is to say that this was the first time in my 43 years to come face to face with death; therefore, I put some deep thought into what I needed to do before I passed. As a Christian, I knew where I was going should I die, yet as a young mother of two children, I wasn't ready.

Strangely, the process of actually planning my funeral was an excellent way for me to be alone with my thoughts and to examine my life to that point. The questions of "Who am I? What legacy will

I leave for my children and grandchildren? and "What impact have I made on this earth for God's kingdom?" needed to reconciled and dealt with.

Processing these deep thoughts and emotions allowed me to reach deep inside myself and cut through the pride and examine the things that don't mean a hill of beans. For the first time in my life, I was laser-focused on just me, myself, and I, and of course, with God. I found the process very peaceful.

What impact have I made on this earth for God's kingdom?

I made it through the surgery as the doctors discovered that the tumor was attached to my spinal cord but was not a non-Hodgkin's lymphoma tumor. On the one hand, the news was good, yet I would need another surgery to remove the remains of the tumor from my spinal cord.

Now having two major surgeries within a few months of one another, I spent a lot of time in bed recovering. I've shared with many people about this period in recovery. Although the time on your back of only looking up could feel daunting, I felt closer to God than I ever have. Months of being still allowed my body to heal and allowed me to talk to God like I've never experienced before.

I was also able to continue down the self-connection path I had begun on the night before the surgery. Reflecting on your life and making plans for the future are actually quite rewarding. What I did learn during this time was how to be still and how to listen intently to God.

I also vowed never to allow my life to become so busy that I didn't have time for God. I also redirected my goals and aspirations to include how I would honor God with the time I did have left on this earth. I prayed earnestly He would show me the path He wanted me on.

After fully recovering over a year later, life was not all peaches and cream. Sadly, my marriage of 21 years ended, and seven years later, a second tumor was discovered in my chest, and this one was in my left lung. I remember telling God I didn't need any more testimony-building experiences.

I'll share more on the lung-tumor experience later on in this book. My point is not to wait for a significant life-altering experience to connect deeply to yourself or to God. It's okay to take time to journal thoughts, spend time alone, and think. You need it, so give yourself permission.

We will dig much more in-depth in Chapter 36 regarding healing and self-forgiveness. For now, merely accepting who you are right now is a massive step in maintaining a healthy and connected relationship within yourself. If you struggle with this, go to the Almighty in prayer and ask Him to help reveal what you need to do to let some things go and to be able to accept yourself as He created you.

CHAPTER 10

GOD'S DIVINE CYCLES

A SERIES of events repeating in the same order over and over is called a cycle. There are many examples of various cycles repeated on the earth, in outer space, and within our bodies. Cyclical mechanisms are perfectly orchestrated systems that ensure sustainable life for us.

Cycles are another fantastic example of the ideally ordered world in which we live and are critical to maintaining life as we know it. They are extremely organized systems when they are correctly functioning unless there is a disruption within the cycle.

Let's take a look at the cycle of photosynthesis. When I was searching for an illustrative point for Theosynthesis, photosynthesis came to mind as the perfect illustration regarding cycles. A cycle will perform adequately when all of the necessary parts or systems are in place and are fully operational.

With photosynthesis, the sun provides the necessary fuel for the plant to create food. The plant takes in carbon dioxide, and in turn, creates life-giving oxygen. This beautiful cycle continues over and over again. If the photosynthetic cycle were to cease, life on earth would come to an abrupt halt.

Within our body systems are many cycles continually working to keep our bodies functioning correctly. Our cells are continuously going through the cycle of division, thus making new cells. Sleep cycles help us to maintain health. Women experience menses cycles during childbearing years.

When any part of a cycle becomes broken or malfunctions, the cycle cannot continue. As I began to write this book, I kept going back to the importance of these fantastic cycles that surrounds our lives. Theosynthesis is one of those cycles we must also recognize as viable to our well-being and work to maintain.

Just as God ordered the world and the living, created organisms, His cycle of design for us is to maintain a connection with Him. When we recognize the cycles of spiritual, emotional, and physical health, it is easy to see this connection within His design.

With Theosynthesis, this connection of the mind, body, and soul provides a perfect example of how God created and designed cycles. If one part of the Theosynthesis cycle is missing, the other parts suffer, and the cycle is not complete. Therein, lies the God-gap.

Even our sleep cycle plays a huge role in our overall well-being. The lack of sleep has enormous and detrimental effects on humans. As we become busier and busier, we deny our bodies and minds the needed sleep and rest required to maintain a healthy and fully functioning body. Sleep deprivation disrupts many of the necessary cycles within our bodies. Without proper sleep, the results are not good. I discuss the importance of rest in further detail in Chapter 25.

With Theosynthesis, this connection of the mind, body, and soul provides a perfect example of how God created and designed cycles. If one part of the Theosynthesis cycle is missing, the other parts suffer, and the cycle is not complete. Therein, lies the God-gap.

Let's place these elements into a triangle to illustrate the cycle of Theosynthesis:

SPIRITUAL: God the Creator (Mind)

PHYSICAL: represents Christ, who came to us in a physical form (Body)

EMOTIONAL: represents the Holy Spirit, who comes to us in the spiritual form. (Soul)

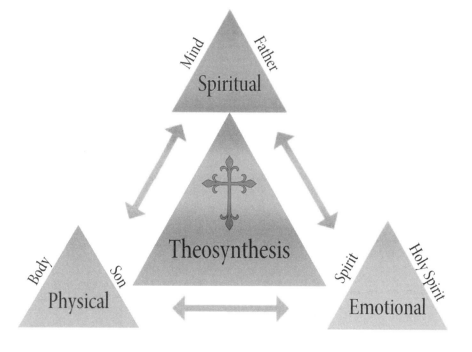

This perfect Triune cycle is how God designed us to maintain balance in our lives. When one or more areas of this cycle are ignored, problems begin to appear. Often, we know something is off, yet we continue to blast forward with our lives without ever working to take care of the missing piece, or should I say, "peace."

Let's take a look at the mind-body-spirit (M-S-B) connection. In many secular spiritual practices are many references regarding the mind, body, and spirit. These parts of the spirit referred to in the secular practice is not the same spirit we see as Christians.

Let's examine the sections of the Theosynthesis Cycle in a bit more detail:

THE MIND

The mind and brain stay in optimal condition by engaging in continuous learning activities. Often, people believe that when they are out of school, maintaining a constant and lifelong learning mode is no longer necessary. For many, they don't see the importance of exercising the brain.

On the contrary, God created the human brain to remain sharp throughout our lives. By maintaining optimal brain health, we must have a healthy, clean diet, proper rest, and limit our exposure to inorganic chemicals and toxins as much as possible. The brain, like any other organ in our body, requires optimal care. If the mind does not stay sharp, the M-B-S connection is broken.

THE BODY

The physical body must also be carefully maintained. In Chapter 24, we will go into great detail on this critical topic. Overall health and well-being of the physical body is critically important. In American, we are witnessing a rapid decline in overall health and wellness.

As we become increasingly sedentary, eat foods that do not nourish our cells properly, the body responds by becoming sick. As the body works hard to fight the onslaught of non-nutritious and cell-damaging substances, disease is the result.

THE SPIRIT

The spirit section of the cycle is more difficult for many to wrap their heads around. We can see and feel bodies, and we know we have a control center, the brain. However, the spirit connection is not so clearly defined or easy to comprehend.

I believe the spirit connection is what we "feel" deeply within our hearts. As discussed in Chapter 7 regarding the illustration of the umbilical cord to God, this is where the spirit connection comes in. This all-important spiritual connection is our responsibility and is essential to our overall well-being.

God ordered this earth and our bodies in a fantastic cyclical manner. The more I discover through my research, the evidence of how perfectly orchestrated both land and life are, the more in awe I am of our intelligent designer. He knew what He was doing when He created us and this beautiful world in which we live.

The cycles of life serve an essential purpose. You are made for a purpose. As you cycle through this life, give Him every part of yourself. Embrace the whole cycle of Theosynthesis as you begin to understand how vital it is for you. I pray you will find peace with Christ.

THEOSYNTHESIS®

PART III
UTILIZING GOD'S POWER & ENERGY

CHAPTER 11

HARNESSING GOD'S ENERGY

WHAT DOES IT MEAN to harness energy? To know this, we first have to understand what the term energy means. Let's take a quick science lesson regarding energy.

Energy is the ability to do work. The definition is the power derived from the utilization of physical or chemical resources, primarily to provide light and heat or to power machines.

The laws of physics regarding energy states:

The Law of Conservation of Energy or the First Law of Thermodynamics:[1] The total energy of an isolated system remains constant. Energy can, of course, transform from one form to another, yet it cannot be created or destroyed.

Energy is converted to other forms through mechanical energy (energy of motion); heat energy such as friction; chemical energy we

---

1   Allison Campbell, Jordan Hanania, James Jenden, Jason Donev. https://energyeducation.ca/encyclopedia/Law_of_conservation_of_energy. University of Calgary, April 28, 2020.

see in our bodies; potential energy (stored energy), which can be released; kinetic energy from movement; and electrical energy that can convert into heat or mechanical energy.

The one form of energy scientists will not recognize, however, is the energy received from God. As I have illustrated in earlier chapters, the Bible is full of verses regarding God's power or power received directly from God. God's power then is another form of energy.

Interestingly, the theory of a big bang has been around for a long time.[2] Recently, scientists became very interested in this theory. But remember, a theory is not a law because the theory has not been proven. As a result, one should remain open-minded to other schools of thought when presented with a new way of thinking.

Scientists have been giddy over this theory of the big bang that pointed to one massive cosmic explosion. What I find interesting is that these scientists will whole-heartedly jump all over an argument such as this one, yet they will scoff at anyone who believes in a Creator. It truly baffles my mind how the big bang parallels with the "in the beginning" statement.

The big bang theorizes that cosmic circumstances caused the subatomic particles and matter to suddenly explode out of nowhere, thus creating the early universe. How and why this could have happened are only theories. For many, it's easier to believe a cosmic big bang than in a God with an intelligent mind.

Yes, there was a big bang, and it is called Creation! Again, the more science uncovers and discovers, the more it all points to our Intelligent Designer. Either way, you choose to believe, both

---

2   Elizabeth Howell, https://www.space.com/25126-big-bang-theory.html, November 07, 2017.

concepts take a great deal of faith. The question begs then, which way will you choose to accept?

Within this chapter, we will specifically focus on harnessing the power and energy God provides. We know that energy exists, and we know He created it. We have discussed the types of harnessed energy in our world and how they are utilized. Why then would we not seek ways to harness the most important source of energy which is God?

As I first began studying and focusing on this concept of God's energy, I found it to be a bit concerning at times. There is much information out there regarding human energy fields or chakras as many call them. These kinds of words and subjects have caused many Christian believers to turn away from seeking to understand them, afraid that these topics are ungodly.

Seeing the rise in the popularity of these secular energy practices is one of the reasons I believe God opened the door of Theosynthesis. In my curiosity of all things God, I struggled with my faith while maintaining an open mind as I studied this concept of God's energy.

The more Scriptures I read regarding God's power, the more it became abundantly clear. Because all energy initially came from God, there is absolutely nothing wrong or scary about exploring God's energy through a different lens. Observing all things through the eyes of God might just allow us to see things in a new light.

The book of John opens with the discussion of light. As we know, light is a form of energy.

"In the beginning, was the Word, and the Word was with God, and the Word was God. He was with God in the beginning. Through Him, all things were made; without Him, nothing was

made that has been made. In Him was life, and that life was the light of men. The light shines in the darkness, but the darkness has not understood it" (John 1:1–5).

Verse 4 states, *"In Him was life, and that life was the LIGHT of men."* There it is, *the* energy source—light which is referring to God Himself. Therefore, God is light and energy as He created it. This light source is given to us through Jesus Christ. Jesus is the light of the world.

"Jesus said, 'I am the light of the world. Whoever follows Me will never walk in darkness, but will have the light of life'" (John 8:12).

What a powerful verse! Our light and energy source are clearly stated right there by Jesus Himself. He goes on with the promise to each of us, that if we choose to follow Him, then we too will possess this same light.

Friends, you will find verse after verse throughout the Bible referencing this exact principle. God has provided a direct light and energy source available for us. All we must to do is simply tap into that wonderful power source.

How then do we tap into God's energy source? We know plants harness sunlight in photosynthetic cells. We also understand nuclear power, electric power, magnetic power, hydropower, wind power, solar power, chemical power, and vibrational power. To harness or use a power source, we must first understand its properties.

God's character or properties are understood when we take the time needed to know Him. Have you ever met a person you were instantly attracted to or perhaps just the opposite, there was something about them that repelled you? Maybe you even said, "I just had a strange vibe from that person."

What you just experienced was real, vibrational energy you felt from that person. When we speak words or sing a song, the sound travels by sound waves called vibrational frequencies. A sound is a form of energy. Sound then is when air molecules move and collide. They vibrate and create disruptions we call sound waves.

As humans, each of us radiates a certain amount of energy constantly. Our bodies are consistently cranking out heat as they process food and regulate our systems. Humans are naturally living energy powerhouses.

Additionally, our emotions and thoughts also create energy. We don't need any scientific proof to know we can be in tune with another person's emotional energy. Even emotions such as anger, despair, frustration, and sadness all manifest as energy. These emotions can be felt and experienced by others.

Those around us can also feel the emotions of happiness, joy, love, and acceptance. Often, we don't even need to say a word to feel the energy radiating from another individual. Each of these range of emotions carries a specific vibrational frequency.

Scientific studies regarding emotions show that our feelings and thoughts have a direct impact on our overall health. People who emit negative emotions consistently will be detrimentally affected both physically and mentally over time. Consistent negative emotion is damaging to human beings down to the cellular level.

Positive emotions, on the other hand, are known to create balance and well-being in people. Studies also show the people who manifest and radiate positive, beautiful thoughts and emotions experience more relaxed and balanced lives. These individuals have found methods allowing them to harness and utilize positive energy.

Our thoughts are a powerful force. We indeed are what we think. Focusing on negative thoughts produces negative energy that radiates outwardly and inwardly. On the other hand, positive, happy thoughts radiate the opposite type of energy from within us. As humans, we emit energy and vibrational frequencies from our magnetic field, which envelopes us.

This magnetic field is an invisible force that either attracts or repels other atomic particles. Atomic particles, as we know, contain their nuclear charge. A magnetic field of any given person or object creates a magnetic force on other objects within the same magnetic field. This force is called magnetism.

Scientifically speaking, it is clear that magnetism is indeed a genuine phenomenon. God created us as electromagnetically charged beings. Every neuron or nerve cell within our body contains an electrical charge. These pulsating electric currents are coursing through and around our bodies continuously.

Doctors and scientists use an electroencephalogram (EEG) to detect the electrical activity of the brain. Because our neurological system transmits via electrically, this phenomenon can easily be measured and observed with these types of machines. Electricity produces energy; therefore, our thoughts and emotions have an energy force.

Our cardiac or heart cells are also electrically charged. An EKG or electrocardiogram is used to measure the rhythm of the heart. An EKG is a test which, measures the electrical activity inside our hearts. Cardiac waves occur and are recorded when a cardiac EKG machine is connected to a human.

Isn't it interesting how God created us with our two most powerful organs of the body, the brain and the heart, to run with electrical currents? Therefore, it would make sense that these two organs are completely connected by these electrical currents. This heart-brain connection is a stunning revelation to scientists.

Science has also discovered that the heart is 5,000 times more electrically charged than our brains.[3] Our hearts are the center of everything within our bodies. When you have been hurt emotionally at a deep level, we often say we feel an ache in our hearts.

This wonderfully made electromagnetic system within our bodies delivers the much-needed blood flow throughout our body while the nervous system sends electrical synapses and impulses. With all of this electrical power going on, this energy also radiates outside of our body.

Scientists have coined a term called "entanglement," which refers to this outer electromagnetic field in humans.[4] This entanglement connects to other electromagnetic fields all around us. Our thoughts and emotions affect the people around us.

If science can accept the fact that humans can connect through an electrically charged field, why then is this such a difficult concept to believe humans can also be connected to an Almighty God in much the same way? The only answer appears to be because it involves God. Many scientists ardently refuse to look at anything that includes God.

As we discussed in Chapter 3, I referenced Scripture verse after Scripture verse with evidence of God's power or energy. Because He is the original energy source, doesn't it make logical sense we too are connected to Him energetically? When we spend time with Him, we can feel His presence and become entangled with His power.

---

3   HeartMath Institute ResearchStaff, https://www.heartmath.org/research/science-of-the-heart/energetic-communication/, 2016.

4   Frank Willczek, *Quanta Magazine*, https://www.quantamagazine.org/entanglement-made-simple-20160428/, April 29, 2016.

Yes, we have indeed connected with Him. Because of this connection, we must plug into Him to harness His authoritative energy source. When we disconnect from God, a spiritual current is missing in our lives. Connecting to Him brings us a life force pulsating through every fiber and cell within us.

As we begin connecting to Him via the cycle of Theosynthesis, we harness His unbelievable strength that will sustain us throughout this life. It is only available for those who desire it.

This power we experience via Theosynthesis is not like what most people think of when they hear this word. This form of energy is from God and is unlike anything else in the universe. Most people refer to this term as something that is physically strong.

God's power, however, is stronger than any physical strength. It provides us with a tethered connection to Him through the Holy Spirit, sustaining us in a way only He can provide. A force such as this can only be experienced when a person freely chooses to accept Christ into their lives.

Here are a few Scripture verses to illustrate this point a bit further:

"...the Kingdom of God is within you" (Luke 17:21).

"You however, are controlled not by sinful nature but by the Spirit, if the Spirit of God lives in you" (Romans 8:9).

The belief that once you accept Christ into your life, you will have unlimited physical powers is not what is I am teaching on this topic. Our physical body is only temporary. Someday, this physical body will die. Spiritually, when the body or the soul remains tethered by the Holy Spirit, this entity will be with Jesus eternally.

Many proclaim Christ a meek or weak man because He chose not to fight back when He was being flogged, beaten, and then hung on the cross. Let me ask, though, which takes more strength? Digging in and becoming defiant or humbly accepting your fate and receiving the punishment even in the face of innocence?

The strength Christ exhibited is something that defies our human mind. His power to endure what He did on that cross could have only come through His Father—God. Before his capture in the Garden of Gethsemane, Jesus prayed in great earnest before His Father. This type of strength is an excellent example of Jesus tapping into the energy source through God via prayer. The power He directly received from God sustained Him as He endured the horrors of the cross.

> *"Father, if You are willing, take this cup from Me; yet not My will but Yours be done. An angel from heaven appeared to Him and strengthened Him" (Luke 22:42–43).*

Jesus knew where to find His ultimate power source and, therefore, went directly to It. His was not the type of physical strength to fight off His accusers; He asked to have the ability to endure whatever had to be done. How fantastic that we have the same source from God that Jesus was given?

Life on Earth was never promised to be smooth sailing as a Christian. It is incorrect teaching to be told otherwise. He does guarantee that His followers are under His guidance and that He will bear our burdens with us. We are to call upon Him for strength in our times of need as Jesus did.

One of my favorite verses which, continues to encourage me is Philippians 4:13:

"I can do all things through Christ who strengthens me."

God's power is the type of energy I wish to harness. We can only find it through our Lord and Savior Jesus Christ. He alone supplies us with His much-needed strength, helping us to endure anything we will encounter in this life.

Do you desire to know and harness this type of might and strength? If so, this gift is there for you. All you need to do is earnestly go to Him and ask for the forgiveness of your sins, invite Jesus into your heart, and have a sincere desire to know Him personally.

As you live your new empowered life through Christ, you too will discover a peace that defies any human understanding. As you grow in a more profound knowledge of Him and His Word, He will show you beautiful and amazing truths. Your mind will be renewed, and your Spirit, as it connects to the Almighty Power Source, will be filled with His light and abiding love.

CHAPTER 12

HOMEOSTASIS, THEOSTASIS, & BALANCE

HOMEOSTASIS is a term many of us learned while in high school biology class. The word simply means to be in a state of balance. Throughout nature and within our own perfectly created bodies, there are systems that are continually working to stay regulated and in balance. Our blood pressure, body temperature, pH levels, hormones, heart rate, and respiration are in a constant state of maintaining a specific level of balance.

Anytime a system in our body moves out of balance, it results in illness until the balance is restored. This same principle applies to Theosynthesis. When we choose to disconnect with God, the God-balance system is off. You could then say that we now enter a phase of being spiritually sick.

A spiritually derived person will not receive the benefits of a God-centered wholeness. Just as the body requires balance, the spirit also requires a balance. A continued connection with God only achieves this balance. A God-centered balance provides believers with a peace that defies all understanding as so beautifully written by Paul in Philippians 4:7:

"And the peace of God, which transcends all understanding, will guard your hearts and your minds in Christ Jesus"

The forces in nature are also always at work, trying to maintain balance. Weather patterns demonstrate that a clear evidence of the water cycle is continuously striving to stay in balance. When the water cycle is out of balance, nature is disturbed. The results are droughts and horrific weather events that result in disturbances and possibly destruction.

As we focus on the homeostatic state within our bodies, it is essential to point out what a huge issue this is in the United States. As humans continue to make poor choices regarding health and wellness, the need to return the body into balance is necessary.

Billions of dollars are spent in the medical industry, working to discover ways to balance our bodies through chemistry. Most of the imbalances experienced today in regards to health are directly associated with the disruptions of balance as a result of nutritional deficits, lack of exercise, and increased stress.

When we then become ill due to neglecting our health and poor food choices, we turn to a doctor expecting them to make us better instantly. As we continue to ignore our health year after year, most will head straight to a doctor and receive a prescription drug to "fix" the problem. Rather than examining the choices and behaviors that resulted in the imbalances and making positive changes, the medical industry responds by treating the symptoms. However, this does not correct the action that caused the disruption of balance in the first place.

After graduating from college armed with a degree in biology, I entered the fledgling new arena of health and fitness. During the early '80s, the country was on the cutting edge of this new concept of health and wellness. I began my career working with a group of twelve physicians in a preventive medicine center in Las Colinas, Texas.

Our focus was on assessing individuals through a myriad of tests to determine their current state of health. We compiled blood tests, muscular-skeletal assessments, cardiac stress testing, body fat measurement, as well as assessing their current diet and stress level. The main goal was obtaining as much information as we could of their state of health at that moment.

This information would then be entered into a computer allowing us to produce a comprehensive report for our clients. The reports focused on areas of weakness and imbalances. This data could then help predict what their future risk could be in developing a significant illness.

With the results in hand, we were able to consult our clients on practical methods they could employ to improve their current state of health. By identifying high-risk areas, we were able to target these concerns and make a plan for them to grow and to maintain optimal health in the future.

Thirty-five years ago, I was blessed to be a part of this new approach to health and wellness. This knowledge has had a tremendous impact on my life. Early on, I recognized the importance of caring for my body, which has been paramount throughout my life.

Three decades later, this early interest in health and wellness helped spark the missing link. Although many people continually strive for the ultimate physical perfection, there is a missing link, a connection to God. This thought is what ultimately gave birth to the term Theosynthesis.

The thought of the whole connection of complete health and wellness with God in the mix just hit me like a ton of bricks.

Striving to achieve the best balance in our lives through diet and exercise will never be enough. Without God, we can never be fully balanced or maintain correct homeostasis, or should I say, a state of Theostasis.

As many in this world continue to deny that God exists, choosing to block Him from their lives will ultimately create an imbalance in one way or another. Without the God-designed balance of Theosynthesis, one will continually strive to maintain a balance in their lives. With the absence of God, however, I would venture to guess if you were to look deeply into their lives, you would find confusion, anger, and distrust, along with an overall fear of death.

I am not saying that those who do know God won't experience those same emotions. We are in a fallen and imperfect world. The big difference then is in how a believer versus a nonbeliever can manage these same emotions. Being able to go directly to God with your problems, your fears, your joys, and your pain can alleviate much of the stress in a way nonbelievers will never know or be able to comprehend.

How many people do you know who experience unique peace in their lives? I would bet those who indeed are at peace with God and maintain a devout, prayerful, and worshipful life. There is no true peace without God at the center of our lives.

I first want to finish this chapter on homeostasis by digging a bit deeper regarding the discussion concerning balance within our diets and exercise. These topics are too important to gloss over. Far too often we place what is essential regarding life on everything else except what fuels our bodies.

As we have discussed, God has already placed everything we need to survive on this earth. Unfortunately, as man continues to destroy and pillage the earth's natural resources and to disrupt the natural cycles of the planet, the result is a polluted planet littered with toxic wastes. These toxins seep into the soil, our water sources, and of course, the air we breathe.

Over years of exposure to these waste products, they eventually seep into our bodies. These toxins become deeply embedded within our tissues and cells and are destroying us from the inside out. Chemical toxins alter our cells down to the DNA level.

The evidence of a toxic environment is all around us. Our precious earth is being destroyed in front of us daily. Why then are we not demanding this madness be stopped? Why are we allowing toxic substances to be added needlessly to food and medicine, which in turn, are making us sick?

Taking a step further to drill down to the crux of this problem, we must look at greed. Plain and simple, the desire of many businesses to make an almighty dollar has helped to perpetuate a world of toxic soup.

If you disagree with the statements above, why on Earth are the products we use on our bodies daily filled with extremely toxic chemicals? Over the years, as many product manufacturers have sought out ways to increase profit margins, the result has been an increase in fillers and additives to these products. These additives allow for the product to go further and to remain on the store and warehouse shelves longer.

Unfortunately, these additives are not the type of substances that benefit the human body. They contain plastics, petroleum products, and a whole myriad of other toxins that do not serve our bodies well. These substances do not only cycle through our bodies; they become stored within our cells.

After years of exposure to these toxins, they become deeply embedded within our cells and organs. As a result, we become sick. Cancer, as we all know, has killed millions and millions of people. It begins at the cellular level when the mechanism for cellular growth goes haywire. After years of toxic exposure, a once normally dividing cell cycle begins to malfunction and doesn't turn off. The cell goes haywire and continues to divide out of control, thus creating a tumorous growth we call cancer.

Healthy cells naturally divide and have a mechanism that turns off once the cell has divided. When the DNA deep within the nucleus of the cell becomes damaged, the cell goes nuts and does not turn off. Cancer cells then begin to proliferate the body and most likely will result in eventual disease and death.

As we ingest, breathe, and bathe ourselves in toxins, these chemicals run through our entire system and begin building up over the years. This build-up of toxic sludge eventually damages us down at the cellular level as mentioned earlier. It may take years for some people to become sick, while others may take very little time in which the disease begins to manifest. Additionally, toxicity levels go up and are subsequently passed to each generation after that.[1]

We know today the level of chemicals within our bodies is almost three times or more than what our ancestors experienced in a lifetime. Why then are we surprised to see cancer rates continuing to increase at alarming rates? Our bodies were simply not designed to handle the massive amounts of chemicals we face today.

---

1 Sen, A., Heredia, N., Senut, M.*et al.* Multigenerational epigenetic inheritance in humans: DNA methylation changes associated with maternal exposure to lead can be transmitted to the grandchildren. *Sci Rep***5,** 14466 (2015), https://doi.org/10.1038/srep14466.

Therefore, as the amount of daily toxic exposure mounts, to maintain a balance within our bodies, we must take drastic measures. We must become educated regarding what we will allow into and on our bodies. We must be diligent in understanding the products we choose to use and slather onto our skin. An emphasis on education to bring about awareness to reducing exposure to toxins is exceptionally critical.

Because we all carry toxins in our tissues and cells, consuming foods loaded with nutritional goodness just as God placed them on Earth for us is the best way to begin detoxifying our bodies. Organic food full of the sun's energy is designed perfectly for the type of foods we were meant to eat. These nutrient-rich plants are loaded with the vitamins and minerals we were created to consume.

Unfortunately, we take beautiful, fresh plants, mash them up, overcook them, add chemicals and preservatives, and then store them in cans. Harmful pesticides are sprayed on them, turning the once healthy living food into toxic, dead food. Dead food refers to the highly processed foods that are laden with chemicals and preservatives. When Consumers eat dead food than living food, the homeostatic balance in the body goes on the blitz.

> *Dead food refers to the highly processed foods that are laden with chemicals and preservatives. When Consumers eat more dead food than living food, the body goes on the blitz.*

In the United States, the obesity problem is more severe than it has ever been. I do not for one minute believe we just have a society of people who can't stop eating. The evidence is mounting against the food industry. It has deceived consumers by creating foods heavily enriched with sugar that we don't need and other toxic materials that are making us sick and unhealthy.

The result of the consumption of our dead-food laden diet is a society desperately needing to be well and yet continues to become sicker. The big businesses running our food industry continue to use inferior food sources while looking for ways to mass produce food with long shelf lives.

Again, the need for education is the only way out of this toxic-soup crisis. We must teach people the importance of caring for their bodies through proper nutrition, not fast food, not canned food but the food which comes right out of the ground the way God put it here on Earth for us to eat.

Thankfully, there appears to be an upward trend of people who are sick and tired of being sick and tired. They are reading, learning, and educating themselves on alternative, holistic wellness methods. Some of these methods include eating clean, nontoxic foods, choosing products without toxic chemicals over those filled with sludge, and seeking a meaningful connection with God.

It appears that many people in our out-of-balance world recognize many things are off. They are tired of being misled, lied to, and deceived. Many are seeking new ways to eat and live in this toxic-laden world.

I have been deemed a health nut for most of my life. I am thankful, however, for the early education I received in this area. Finally, many people are waking up and are now desperately seeking alternative methods as they seek better ways to live. I have worked hard to take care of myself in this toxic world. I am thankful to have a healthy body, along with a sincere faith, because both have allowed me to continue on this life journey.

My own life has been significantly affected by exposure to lifelong chemical build-up. I've experienced a massive spinal cord tumor that should have killed me, and at a minimum, should have put me into a wheelchair. Six years later, a rare and massive lung tumor resulted in the subsequent loss of a lung that should have done me in.

After surviving these two rare tumor growths, I completed comprehensive genetics testing from one of the most exceptional medical facilities in the nation. These tests determined that genetics was not the cause of my tumors. Most likely, these tumors developed from chemicals stored in my body over the years. This information ticked me off big time!

This revelation put me on a major quest to begin exploring this area of chemical exposure in my own lives. As a result of this quest, I started pulling out every product I used in my home. Every cleaning and personal-care product I owned now became part of a research project into their ingredients.

What I discovered was astounding! The main culprits I looked for included parabens, triclosan, synthetic colorings, and sodium lauryl.[2] I pulled out a large trash bag where almost every product in my home ended up. My level of anger was at an all-time high.

It was a huge turning point in my life when I discovered that those products I purchased and believed to be safe were poisoning me. I was angry and became more determined than ever to learn all I could regarding these toxins. I felt duped and lied to by not

---

2   https://www.chemicalsafetyfacts.org/parabens/, https://www.ncbi.nlm.nih.gov/pmc/articles/PMC6126357/, https://www.forbes.com/sites/rachelhennessey/2012/08/27/living-in-color-the-potential-dangers-of-artificial-dyes/#76bb4fff107a, https://www.ncbi.nlm.nih.gov/pmc/articles/PMC4651417/

only the companies using these toxins but by the Food and Drug Administration who allows these toxins into our products.

As a result of my findings, I made significant changes in the products I purchased from that moment forward. I now only choose plant-based products with as few preservatives and chemicals as possible. This process has taken quite a bit of research but has been worth the work.

Armed with the knowledge I now have regarding the daily exposure to chemical toxins, I am on a mission to educate as many people as I can. The birth of Theosynthesis came out of this mission as I worked on tweaking my workshops on health and wellness.

Although being involved with health and wellness for the past three decades, my body was silently being attacked. Stealthily, a subtle infiltration of chemicals in my everyday life was wreaking havoc on my body. Eating right and exercising were crucial, yet environmental toxins were making me sick. My body reacted to these toxins by creating large tumors.

We will continue to dig a little deeper into the importance of caring for our precious bodies in Section IV of this book. It's a critical topic that truly requires much more to be said on the subject. I believe you will also understand and see the urgency of the emphasis regarding this subject.

In closing, you may choose to ignore your health, your spiritual wellness, and your level of fitness for a lifetime. However, if you want to follow these paths, you will most likely end up living with at least one, if not numerous secondary diseases as a result of those choices.

On the other hand, you may choose to make some decisions right now to discover living a life of health, wellness, and spiritual wholeness. While this may not be an easy road, it is indeed a personal choice. Destroying your body from the inside out will eventually manifest into some form of a disease and physical distress.

God's Word states that our bodies are a temple. We are given this beautiful body to care for and protect. God commands us to care for our temple. I sincerely hope you will choose to honor your God-given body and decide to consider how very precious you are and to care for yourself.

What are you doing or not doing right now to care for your temple? What will it take to open your eyes to the importance of personal health? Will you take a moment to pray this moment for God to show you exactly what changes you need to make to achieve optimal health and homeostasis?

CHAPTER 13

PRAYER & MEDITATION

WE HAVE TOUCHED on the basics of prayer and meditation in Chapter Four. Because they are such important concepts, they beg for a more in-depth review, so we'll tackle them in this chapter.

Why is it that prayer is often a difficult thing for us to do? Perhaps it is because we may not hear or see any results. Maybe you desperately went to God to answer a request, and He didn't answer the way you had hoped.

Understanding prayer is the first step in learning what prayer is and what it is not. Many times as Christians, we are not taught much about prayer other than it is something we are to do. Too often, we get caught in the trap that prayer requires some unique formula, or we worry we are doing it incorrectly.

The verse says it all:

"Do not be anxious about anything, but in every situation, by prayer and petition, with thanksgiving, present your requests to God. And the peace of God, which transcends all

understanding, will guard your hearts and your minds in Christ
Jesus" (Philippians 4:6–7).

This verse clearly shows that in everything we encounter, we should not be anxious but go to God with our needs. When we go to Him with a thankful and open heart, we are to present to Him our requests. The verse then follows with the assurance that the peace of God, which transcends all understanding, will comfort and guard our hearts and mind.

As believers, this a beautiful promise for us all. We simply lay it all at God's feet and receive His peace. The only way to experience this peace is by spending time with God in intimate and earnest prayer.

The act of prayer then is to simply talk to God. You don't need any formal training to do this. You just need an open heart.

Open Heart:
The ability to be vulnerable, authentic, and accessible. Allowing others to know you deeply and intimately.

What prayer is not is thinking that you can harness God's power for your purposes. Merely going to God with your agenda, demanding He does this or that is not what the Bible teaches about prayer. As we saw from the verse in Luke, where Jesus Himself is crying out to God, He clearly says, "*not My will but Yours*" (Luke 22:42).

By far, this is the most challenging concept for most of us to understand. God is here for us, and we can bring all of our requests to Him, yet He alone decides what He will do with them. When He does not grant our petitions, many lose faith.

However, how many prayers have you given to God that were answered at a later date? Perhaps your prayer was answered in a completely different way than what you expected. We, in our limited and finite minds, cannot possibly know why God chooses to answer or not to answer our prayers the way He does.

What we must hang on to is that He ultimately has our best interest in mind. He also sees the big picture that we cannot. What we may see as an unanswered prayer may be a blessing in disguise. I love Garth Brooks's song, "Unanswered Prayers."

Developing a prayer routine that works for you is crucial. Staying in touch with the Almighty Father takes time on your part. If you desire to tap into the Theosynthesis cycle, you must make time for Him. You must believe that this is as vital as sleeping, eating, and breathing.

A vibrant prayer life incorporated into your daily life will provide you with a deeper connection to God, thus filling the missing God-gap or Theosynthesis gap. Offering God your time and your attention will enrich your life in more ways than you can imagine

I recently heard Pastor Rick Warren on the radio say, "Why would anyone want to spend eternity with God if they never wanted to spend any time with Him while they were here on Earth?" An excellent question, isn't it? Many people believe they can simply live the way they want without any regard to God, and then when they need Him, He will help them.

We can't say that God won't or doesn't answer prayers for anyone who earnestly calls out to Him. Doesn't it make sense then that if you believe He is the ultimate source of life, you would want to spend a lot of time with Him? Why ignore Him until something significant happens?

Having God to lean on during my toughest times has been an anchor for me. I have said this, and I hear others say it all of the time, "I wonder how those without Christ get by when tragedy strikes." Without Him, this must be a very hopeless and scary time.

Yes, there will still be very scary and distressful times, even with Christ in the center. The difference lies in experiencing the peace we can experience as we learn to lean on Him in times of trouble. I know that for me, having this power source in my corner has not only helped me through the difficulties, but I have been profoundly enriched because of this beautiful connection.

> *"And the peace of God, which transcends all understanding, will guard your hearts and your minds in Christ Jesus" (Philippians 4:7).*

This peace does indeed surpass all understanding. Those who have experienced this glorious peace amid unimaginable tragedy understand this. We as mere humans cannot possibly comprehend everything that God is and how He supplies our needs.

There is no magic sauce in how you pray to God. You don't need fancy "Christian-ease" words, nor do you need to know every Scripture in the Bible. A willing heart and a desire to spend time with God are all that is required. Too many people try to make this simple yet essential task way too complicated.

I have immersed myself in a comprehensive, in-depth Bible study for over two decades. One of the greatest things I have learned from it was a good, basic pattern for prayer. This form of worship can serve as an excellent outline for me when I am praying to my Father.

BASIC PRAYER GUIDE

Various prayers are useful at different times of the day. There are those quick "arrow" prayers that you can shoot up at any time when something happens or comes to mind.

The specific and intentional prayer time is what I am referring to in this prayer guide. Remember, this is your time with God. You can explore various manners of prayer and find one that works best for you.

Jesus instructed His Disciples in Matthew 6:9–13, known as the Lord's Prayer. This prayer is a perfect example of an outline of how to pray. Praying the Lord's Prayer is excellent, yet using it as a template is perhaps a better way to organize your petitions.

> *"This, then, is how you should pray: Our Father in heaven, hallowed be Your name, Your kingdom comes, Your will be done, on Earth as it is in heaven. Give us today our daily bread. And forgive us our debts, as we also have forgiven our debtors. And lead us not into temptation, but deliver us from the evil one."*

Let's dissect this a bit further:

OUR FATHER – to whom you are praying

YOUR KINGDOM COMES – obedience to Him

GIVE US THIS DAY – your petitions

FORGIVE – asking for grace and forgiveness for others

DELIVER US – prayer for protection from sinful ways

No matter how you plan to formulate your prayers, having, a plan is a good practice. Remember, you don't need to focus too much on "getting it right." Instead, just start praying and allow God to help you. You will find the more time you spend in prayer, the more comfortable you will become.

The prayer template I enjoy using follows this typical pattern:

PRAISE

I begin with words of praise to God the Father. I honor Him with words of His attributes. I may say some of the following phrases:

"You, oh Lord, are the Most-High! You are the Almighty King. You are in control. You are the same yesterday, to-day, and tomorrow."

I praise and honor God for His attributes and acknowledge who He is.

An excellent way to spend time with God is by creating a journal of God's attributes. I have one page per the letter of the alphabet and simply list out His characteristics one word at a time. Not only is this an interesting exercise, but it also serves as a wonderful guide to have when you are in prayer.

PURPOSEFUL THANKSGIVING

Next, my prayer consists of purposefully thanking God for what He has done in my life and the lives of others. I believe in fully recognizing the things for which I am thankful, and this helps me to put my requests and petitions in focus. A grateful heart and attitude are always great ways to spend time with God.

"Thank You, Father, for Your unfailing love. Thank You that You stopped the rain. Thank You, oh Lord, for giving us Your precious Son, Jesus."

If you choose to create a journal of God's attributes, you may want to create another section to record the things you are thankful for in your life. What a perfect way to remind yourself of all He has done for you. I like to get this out when I am down in the dumps. It is a great way to get your mind refocused off of a negative situation.

PETITIONS AND REQUESTS

The final part of my prayer focuses on the issues and requests I am putting before Him—everything on your heart, the people you are praying for, situations, children, and finances, whatever it is that you wish to give to Him. This is where I recognize who God is, thank Him, and finally bring Him my requests.

What is the difference between prayer and meditation? For many in the Christian Church, meditation is not understood clearly and is looked upon as something foreign and not of God. It is easy to see why the term "meditation" has taken on a negative connotation. Many non-Christians, however, meditate to various entities that have nothing to do with God.

The practice of meditation that does not include God has become a taboo topic for many Christians. Meditation is, however, mentioned in the Bible many times. The question begs then, how is meditation different than prayer?

Many people link meditation and yoga practices together. During a yoga session, one is instructed to lie still and not to think. Some methods have you go "inward" to your secret place. Meditation, in this sense, focuses on elevating humans to a position wherein they are in control over everything in their lives. Some even want to promote themselves devoid of God or to *be* their own God!

God's Word, however, has us focusing on doing all things through Christ. The Scripture in Psalm 46:10 is a beautiful verse reminding us to stop and get out of our busy lives and just listen to God. It requires discipline to carve out time to be quiet before Him.

I find this very challenging to do. My mind is continually racing and just completely stopping to be still and listen to God is difficult. Yet when I do stop and meditate on God, I am instantly relaxed and in a better place. My entire being relaxes while feeling the stress melting away.

Being still is being in an awake yet resting state. Allowing ourselves to take a moment to relax and reflect is the goal. When we do this and focus our mind on God, He will communicate with us in unexpected ways. When we are quiet, we can then be able to hear Him.

"Be still and know that I am God" (Psalm 46:10).

Prayer and meditation, therefore, are two different activities. Both are God-centered; however, prayer is going to Him while meditation is allowing Him to come to you.

As we close this chapter, I hope that you will take a moment to meditate on your prayer life right now. What do you need to do to have your prayer time be more meaningful?

What time-wasting activities could you give up to enter into a powerful time of prayer each day?

I believe that once you incorporate prayer and meditation into your life, you will find that your stress level will go down. You will find a balance. Yes, my friend, you will begin to experience the Theosynthesis aspect of your life that will fill a void like none other. The God-gap will close as you learn to bask in the beauty of prayer.

CHAPTER 14

WORSHIP

THE TERM WORSHIP has many different meanings for various people. Additionally, there are varying views of worship. This term can be used in a positive form or in a negative manner, such as worshipping a lifestyle, a movie star, money, or even dark or evil entities.

The Merriam-Webster Dictionary defines "worship" as:

Noun—the feeling or expression of reverence and adoration for a deity.

Verb—show reverence and adoration for (a deity); honor with religious rites.

Regarding God, there are many ways to worship Him. The Bible states we are to worship God alone. Defining the deity of God is the most crucial aspect of worship. In Exodus 34:14, God tells us not to worship any other god.

"Jesus answered, "It is written: 'Worship the Lord your God and serve Him only" (Luke 4:8).

Worship must first begin within the heart of each believer. When one truly adores their Lord and Savior, they will naturally desire to bow before Him. A believer will want to show their adoration to their Lord.

A humble attitude of putting yourself beneath God is the only way to prepare to worship Him. As we've discussed in previous chapters, God doesn't make us do anything we don't want to. Therefore, this humility must be something a believer feels led to do.

When we as believers come before God reverently and with respect, this demonstrates the ultimate act of love toward Him. We are saying to Him, "Father, You are my God. You are worthy of all praise. You are above everything else." The main point being, we must approach Him out of respect for Him as Lord.

The Bible does not give us an exact example of how to worship. It does provide us with many references on excellent ways to praise our Lord, which include prayer, song, Bible study, corporate worship, and spending quiet time before only the Lord. Sadly, many churches have placed unnecessary rules and restrictions of how and when we should worship, thereby creating division amongst believers.

We should go to church and worship. The Ten Commandments in Exodus 20:8 says, "Remember the Sabbath day by keeping it holy." Clearly God has commanded His believers to set a day aside to worship Him.

We cannot become dogmatic in believing that Sunday is the *only* day to worship God. In the United States, Sunday was set aside as the day Christians would attend church. Many churches have Saturday services and other services throughout the week. The most crucial point is in finding time to worship.

Historically, the Hebrew word for "Sabbath" is *shavath*, which means "to stop" or "to cease." God commanded us to rest, and on that day of rest, spend time in worship of Him. God, in His infinite wisdom, knows we need time to rest our minds and our bodies from our work. We know what happens when we don't take time to rest completely.

Without proper rest, the human body becomes more susceptible to illness and disease. Our minds don't function as well, and we tend to make more mistakes. Today, our schedules are busier than ever! Many people pride themselves on packing their calendar full of meetings, activities, and events.

Continuously filling our lives with everything but God, we then find we have no time to spend with Him at all. I know I am guilty of this. What I have continued to discover time and again is when I do get too busy for God, my life begins to become frazzled and hectic.

When I choose to leave God out of my life, I inherently know I need to just stop and focus on Him. He created us with the desire to spend time with Him. Just as we need food and water, we need Him in our lives.

Leaving God out decreases our intimate connection, Theosynthesis, with Him; thereby, we become out of balance with our Creator. When things begin spinning out of control, we must find our way back to Him. When we don't take time for God, we get into trouble.

Just for a moment, reflect on what happens when there is a national disaster, the sudden loss of a close friend or family member, the devastating news of cancer. Most people sink to their knees and cry out to God during these times, even if they have placed Him on the back burner previously. There is an innate need to pray and cry out to God.

There are many stories of nonbelievers who became ardent believers after a big wake-up call. Why then do many have to wait for disaster to strike before reaching out to God? Arrogance, indifference, and perhaps defiance are all reasons we often disregard Him.

Whether we choose to admit it or not, our DNA is designed to seek out God, to know Him, and to ultimately decide to worship Him. How we get to that place of worship is up to each one of us individually. Ignoring Him or depending on our power will prove time and time again to be ultimately futile.

Is there any right or wrong way to then worship? This topic is where many believers become divided. Take a look at some examples from Scripture where God is glorified:

WE ARE CALLED TO GLORIFY THE LORD

"O LORD, our Lord, how majestic is your name in all the earth! You have set your glory above the heavens" (Psalms 8:1).

"Ascribe to the LORD the glory due his name; worship the LORD in the splendor of holiness" (Psalms 29:2).

"Oh come, let us worship and bow down; let us kneel before the LORD, our Maker!" (Psalms 95:6).

"Exalt the LORD our God; worship at his footstool! Holy is he!" (Psalms 99:5).

"Jesus said to her, 'Woman, believe me, the hour is coming when neither on this mountain nor in Jerusalem will you

worship the Father. You worship what you do not know; we worship what we know, for salvation is from the Jews. But the hour is coming, and is now here, when the true worshipers will worship the Father in spirit and truth, for the Father is seeking such people to worship him. God is spirit, and those who worship him must worship in spirit and truth.'" (John 4:21–24).

God desires us to worship Him. He isn't demanding we worship Him; He simply yearns for us to spend time with Him. Wow, the Lord of the universe desires to spend time with you and with me. What a powerful truth!

When we go before God in humble worship, He fills us with an undeniable energy force. This force is the heart of Theosynthesis! We connect our lives with the Almighty to give Him our hearts and our thoughts through a worshipful experience. As a result, we come away with a renewed spirit, mind, and body.

Clearly God desires us to worship Him. He isn't demanding we worship Him; He simply yearns for us to spend time with Him. Wow, the Lord of the universe desires to spend time with you and me! This alone is a powerful truth.

The Scriptures clearly demonstrate that we are called to worship. God is Holy and therefore, worthy of all our worship and praise. Praising God reminds me of the song, "Oh Come Let Us Adore Him."

WHY WE SHOULD WORSHIP

"*But you shall seek the place that the LORD your God will choose out of all your tribes to put His name and make his habitation there. There you shall go, and there you shall bring your burnt offerings and your sacrifices, your tithes and the contribution that you present, your vow offerings, your freewill offerings, and the firstborn of your herd and of your flock. And there you shall eat before the LORD your God, and you shall rejoice, you and your households, in all that you undertake, in which the LORD your God has blessed you*" (Deuteronomy 12:5–7).

"*Therefore God has highly exalted him [Jesus] and bestowed on him the name that is above every name, so that at the name of Jesus every knee should bow, in heaven and on earth and under the earth, and every tongue confess that Jesus Christ is Lord, to the glory of God the Father*" (Philippians 2:9–11).

"*Draw near to God, and He will draw near to you*" (James 4:8).

"*And they sang a new song, saying, "Worthy are You to take the scroll and to open its seals, for You were slain, and by your blood, You ransomed people for God from every tribe and language and people and nation*" (Revelation 5:9).

"*Worthy are You, our Lord and God, to receive glory and honor and power, for You created all things, and by Your will they existed and were created*" (Revelation 4:11).

EXAMPLES OF WORSHIP

"Then Moses entered the tent, the pillar of cloud would descend and stand at the entrance of the tent, and the LORD would speak with Moses. And when all the people saw the pillar of cloud standing at the entrance of the tent, all the people would rise up and worship, each at his tent door" (Exodus 33:9–10).

"Enter His gates with thanksgiving, and His courts with praise! Give thanks to Him; bless His name!" (Psalms 100:4).

"I appeal to you therefore, brothers, by the mercies of God, to present your bodies as a living sacrifice, holy and acceptable to God, which is your spiritual worship. Do not be conformed to this world, but be transformed by the renewal of your mind, that by testing you may discern what is the will of God, what is good and acceptable and perfect" (Romans 12:1–2).

"I have been crucified with Christ. It is no longer I who live, but Christ who lives in me. And the life I now live in the flesh I live by faith in the Son of God, Who loved me and gave Himself for me" (Galatians 2:20).

"In the days of his flesh, Jesus offered up prayers and supplications, with loud cries and tears, to Him who was able to save him from death, and He was heard because of his reverence" (Hebrews 5:7).

Isn't it clear from the Scriptures, God designed us to know and to seek Him? By correctly aligning with God, we then desire to be in worship with Him. This act of worship fuels our souls and helps to ease the anguish we experience in life.

When we stray from God, imbalances in our lives become apparent. We know we need to bow down and give ourselves to God. First, however, we must humble ourselves before Him.

What prevents us then, from just letting go and letting God? Shouldn't worship then be a spontaneous activity? The answer is yes, it should be, yet the world would like to keep you and me busy, distracted, and stressed out. The busier we are, the easier it is to take our focus off of the Almighty Creator.

Because we live in a hyperstressed-out society, people in our world today continue to seek ways to destress. Many may simply run away from their problems. Others turn to mind-numbing alternatives such as drugs, alcohol, gambling, or sex to escape their pain.

These are terrible cycles we continue to see repeating again and again. It doesn't have to be this way if people would just understand all they need to do is to connect with the highest of sources—God. He has just what each of us needs if we would only turn to Him. Connecting to God through worship, prayer, meditation, and God-honoring music will fill us to the brim with an energizing frequency that can be matched by nothing else.

WORSHIP THROUGH SONG AND MUSIC

"Then Miriam the prophetess, the sister of Aaron, took a tambourine in her hand, and all the women went out after her with tambourines and dancing. And Miriam sang to them: 'Sing to the LORD, for he has triumphed gloriously; the horse and his rider he has thrown into the sea'" (Exodus 15:20–21).

"But I will sing of your strength; I will sing aloud of your stead-fast love in the morning. For you have been to me a fortress and a refuge in the day of my distress" (Psalms 59:16).

"The heavens declare the glory of God, and the sky above pro-claims his handiwork" (Psalms 63:3–4).

"All the earth worships you and sings praises to you; they sing praises to your name" (Psalms 66:4).

"Praise the LORD! Praise God in his sanctuary; praise him in his mighty heavens! Praise him for his mighty deeds; praise him accord-ing to his excellent greatness! Praise him with trumpet sound; praise him with lute and harp! Praise him with tambourine and dance; praise him with strings and pipe! Praise him with sounding cym-bals; praise him with loud clashing cymbals! Let everything that has breath praise the LORD! Praise the LORD!" (Psalms 150).

Music and singing create a wonderful open heart that allows our souls to richly connect with God. Again, there is no set-in-stone type of music. Music that reaches deeply into your soul and results in a desire to connect with the Almighty is a wonderful experience. I am one of those people who is not musically talented by any means. I do, however, love music and know that certain tones or melodies truly do open me up to a deep and meaningful worship experience.

There are many studies regarding music and the vibrational frequency of musical tones. Our ancestors inherently knew about these healing, connecting, and powerful frequencies that exist be-tween music and man. Today, through science and technology, great strides are occurring in this area.

I have devoted the entire next chapter to the power of musical vibrational frequency. I believe you will find this information quite fascinating. God created everything, so why are we so surprised to find even the beautiful tones of music were created by Him and can be used to heal us both emotionally, spiritually, and physically?

You can watch some outstanding videos regarding the musical tones of plants, animals, even the universe.[1] Take a moment to watch some of these. There is simply no denying our God has His hand in every single thing in this entire universe.

Recently, I listened to a video of the sound crickets make that was dramatically reduced in speed. What blew me away was how absolutely powerful and beautiful the sound was. Imagine all of the different frequencies of various sounds out there we may not even be aware of.

I believe this symphony of music throughout the universe points to God's creation in worship to Him. Wow, what a thought! Even the stars, the plants. and the animals inherently know to worship Him? Why is it, we as humans often find this so difficult?

In closing this chapter, worship is a natural response to God. There is no single method that is right for everyone. Taking time to express to God that you find Him worthy to worship is one of the most critical aspects of your life. Next is showing this love to Him in a way that is meaningful to you and puts Him first.

How will you slow down and find the time in which to worship God? What might you need to give up to free up some time for Him? Reflect on these questions and ask God to help you find meaningful ways to worship Him.

---

1   "God's Crickett Chorus," https://www.youtube.com/watch?v=OP-6JGlv32nw, January 23, 2015.

CHAPTER 15

GOD'S POWER
WE ALL POSSESS

"*TO THIS END* I labor, *struggling with all His energy which so powerfully works in me*" from Colossians 1:29 is marked in my Bible with the word "Theosynthesis" next to it. When God laid the word Theosynthesis on my heart, this particular verse jumped off the page. What a perfect verse to remind us of how God designed us to have His power to work within us!

Theosynthesis then is His energy that powerfully works in me. Yes, this is the message of this entire book. As believers, we also possess this God-energy As I focused on the meaning of this, I was astounded in what this means to believers.

Looking back on Chapter 11 regarding God's energetic radiance, the question I have is, since we are made in His image, do we also embody His energy and His light? The type of energy and light I am referring to are the ones received directly from God. I am not referring to the popular secular definitions of sharing light and love.

In taking this discussion a step further, we can investigate these terms based on the God of the Bible and on whom I am basing this book. What does God have to say about His power residing within His people?

The text from 1 Chronicles 29 is interesting as David knows the work of the temple is about to begin. He says in verse 1, *"Then King David said to the whole assembly: My son Solomon, the one whom God has chosen, is young and inexperienced. The task is great, because this palatial structure is not for man but for the Lord God."*

In verse 12, as part of David's prayer to the Lord, he says, *"Wealth and honor come from You; You are the ruler of all things. In Your hands are strength and power to exalt and give strength to all."*

David was quite wise in recognizing that God *is* the source of strength. He goes on to comprehend that God *gives* this strength to all. This verse quite clearly illustrates the question posed in this chapter, whether our Almighty God does indeed supply us with His wonderful energy source.

The Bible has more than 270-plus verses using the word "power," which clearly demonstrates that this is an attribute of God that He bestows upon His people. As we look closely into many of these verses, I believe you will come to know and understand the abilities you also possess as a child of His. As believers, we have a huge responsibility with this God-given gift. As believers, He requires us to use this source for the glory of His kingdom.

Moses certainly did not part the sea on his own. Instead, he turned to God and allowed God's mighty to be displayed all through him. Exodus 14:21 says, *"Then Moses stretched out his hand over the sea, and all that night the Lord drove the sea, and all that night the Lord drove the sea back with a strong east wind and turned it into dry land."*

If you believe this singular act is not possible, let me ask you this question. Have you ever been to the beach as the wind pushes in from the opposite direction from the waves? The wind pushing against the waves can be greater than the force of those waves and will push the water back from the shore. Seeing this is quite a phenomenon and is a great visual reminder of the strength the wind can bring forth.

As we observe many weather events and other fascinating natural events on earth, we can see these forces displayed in remarkable ways. Because God is the Creator of all of these events, why would it be impossible for Him to use these events to show His power and to achieve His will? God is God, and nothing is beyond His capability.

When I finally committed to finishing this book, I was able to go to Destin, Florida, and stay in the home of some dear friends. The very first day I arrived and went to the beach. I saw the effects of the wind pushing against the waves firsthand. At first, I couldn't understand why there were so many exposed sandbars, and the sea itself was so far out. Having been to this beach many times and witnessed both high and low tides, I had never seen this much of the shoreline exposed before.

Finally, I recognized what was happening. Because I was there in January, and a strong, northerly wind was bearing down on the Gulf, the wind was holding back the waves. It was fascinating to witness. This event provided the perfect visual for imagining God's mighty strength when He held the water back in the Red Sea for the Israelites.

Let's head back to the Scriptures to take a look at what else God has to say about Him providing His people with His power:

"*The God of Israel gives* **power** *and strength to His people*" (Psalm 68:35).

"*But those who hope in the Lord will renew their* **strength**" (Isaiah 39:31).

"But as for me, I am filled with **power**, with the Spirit of the Lord" (Micah 3:8).

"But you will receive **power** when the Holy Spirit comes on you" (Acts 1:8).

"With great **power**, the apostles continued to testify to the resurrection of the Lord Jesus" (Acts 4:33).

"Now Stephen, a man full of God's grace and **power**, did great wonders and miraculous signs among the people" (Acts 6:8).

"May the God of hope fill you with all joy and peace as you trust in Him, so that you may overflow with hope by the **power** of the Holy Spirit" (Romans 15:13).

"My message and my preaching were into with wise and persuasive words, but with a demonstration of the Spirit's **power**, so that your faith might not rest on men's wisdom, but on God's **power**" (1 Corinthians 2:4–5).

"But He said to me, 'My grace is sufficient for you, My **power** is made perfect in weakness'..." (2 Corinthians 12:9).

"And His incomparably great **power** for us who believe. ..." (Ephesians 1:19).

"Finally, be strong in the Lord and in His mighty **power**" (Ephesians 6:10)

"Who through faith, are shielded by God's **power**" (1 Peter 1:5).

These are but a few of the many verses in the Bible we find on the subject of God's power that He bestows it on us, His believers. Let's break down these various uses of this word:

POWER AS A GIFT

Over and over in the Scriptures, we see examples of God giving His children the gift of His power. The people of Israel during the exodus and in the Book of Acts during the Pentecost demonstrates the gift of the Holy Spirit given to believers.

> *"Peter replied, 'Repent and be baptized, every one of you, in the name of Jesus Christ for the forgiveness of your sins. And you will receive the gift of the Holy Spirit'" (Acts 2:38).*

Recognizing this strength from God is a gift, we should be overflowing with gratefulness as we thank Him for it. We should never take this gift with a grain of salt. As a believer, when we do things in His name, we all possess the gift of the Holy Spirit within us.

Therefore, shouldn't we stop doubting ourselves when called to do something in His kingdom? If we believe the power of the Holy Spirit is indwelling within us, this alone should be the encouragement we need to go boldly ahead in whatever work He is leading us to do.

POWER WITHIN BELIEVERS

The verses above use "filled us," "renewed us," and "received." As believers, when we accept Christ in our lives, the Holy Spirit fills us and renews us. A filling means over every square inch of us and within every fiber. God creates us as new creations from the inside out.

> "*May the God of hope fill you with all joy and peace as you trust in Him, so that you may overflow with hope by the* **power** *of the Holy Spirit*" *(Romans 15:13).*

We must also "receive" this gift. Typically, when you receive a gift, you are thankful and express this to the person who gave it to you. Likewise, we as believers must also welcome and receive this beautiful gift from Christ and to tell Him, "Thank you."

POWER AS PROTECTION

God's Word does not say that when we become believers, bad things will stop happening to us. What He does promise is because we are indwelt with His power, He will be with us through whatever we are going through. When we genuinely believe this, and when we do experience the tough times, knowing without a shadow of a doubt that He is with us is more comfortable than anything else we can ever know.

Personally, as I walked through two terrifying illnesses and was told to get my affairs in order, thankfully, as a believer at the time, I was filled with an uncanny peace. Knowing I was never alone, even though I was frightened out of my mind, gave me a peace far beyond my human understanding.

> "*And the peace of God, which transcends all understanding, will guard your hearts and your ends in Christ Jesus.*" *(Philippians 4:7).*

Had I been alone in my thoughts, it would have been easy to give up during this time. However, having an in-depth and convicting knowledge that no matter what the outcome, God was going to lead me through; He was my lifeline. This truth alone truly defies all understanding as we try to comprehend things within our strength.

I love clinging to the knowledge that the same power God used to part the Red Sea and to resurrect Jesus also resides within me. What a fantastic truth! This concept alone should blow your mind!

No doubt, then you, my friend as a believer, can rest in knowing without a shadow of a doubt, every cell and tissue within you is woven tightly together with the power of our beloved Jesus Christ. I can think of no better promise as we confidently put our faith and hope in Him. Rest in this knowledge and ask Him to undergird you with His confidence in this power.

Ask Him to show you this power in a personal way and how He desires for you to utilize it. What beautiful things would you be capable of if you genuinely comprehended that you possess the power of the Holy Spirit? This thought alone has been life-changing in my life.

CHAPTER 16

RADIATING GOD'S LOVE & LIGHT

THE SONG "Shine" by the Newsboys came to mind as I began working on this chapter. Many years ago, as contemporary praise and worship music was just beginning to come on to the scene, the song "Shine" by the Newsboys was a favorite of mine. The main chorus focuses on shining before all men and to glorify the Lord.

The word "shine" means to emit rays of light, to be bright by the reflection of light, or to have a bright, glowing appearance. The Bible is jammed packed with verses on light that refer to these definitions. Whenever God, Jesus, or the Holy Spirit is described, they are frequently described in some way in describing light.

Other words and phrases such as radiance, glow, a brilliance, a beam, and a ray are also commonly found when we read about God's presence. I have been fascinated by God's light from the first time I watched the original movie *The Ten Commandments*. Moses comes off of Mount Sinai after meeting with God, and his hair is a brilliant white while having a look of awe and wonder deeply etched into his face.

Of course, this was Hollywood's version of this incident, yet the Scriptures clearly describe what happened. In Exodus 34:29,

"*When Moses came down from Mount Sinai with the two tablets of the covenant law in his hands, he was not aware that his face was radiant because he had spoken with the Lord.*" His face was radiant!

Further down in this passage, we see anytime Moses would go into the tent and talk to God, he would come out with his face so exceedingly radiant that he put on a veil in front of the people. There was no doubt the people of Israel knew and understood something was visibly different about Moses. His inner light was shining, and it was noticeable.

The term Shekinah Glory comes from the Hebrew language meaning the presence of God dwelling on Earth. Many believe the pillar of light that guided the Israelites throughout their journey through the desert was an example of God's Shekinah Glory. This type of light, however, is not the type of light we are familiar with here on Earth.

Just as sound consists of frequencies, light also has a type of frequency that can be measured. The Shekinah Glory light doesn't appear to follow the laws of light as we know. This light is different. It is brilliant yet isn't blinding. Science has not yet been able to define this type of light.

Science has discovered something they call the Kirlian effect.[1] This phenomenon is a visible electrophotonic glow of an object in response to a pulsed electrical field excitation. In layman's terms, this simply means there is a glow, or as some call it, an aura of light surrounding an object. Extraordinary photographs can capture this glow around various objects.

---

1 Dr. Christopher S. Baird, Do Kirlian Photographs Show the Soul of an Organism?, https://wtamu.edu/~cbaird/sq/2016/02/10/do-kirlian-photographs-show-the-soul-of-an-organism/, February 10, 2016.

Some scoff at this effect as nothing more than light from water vapor of the object, while others believe there is more to this. We have discussed the science of energy and light; therefore, it makes sense to me that living objects can also emit light from within as it utilizes the power within.

The stronger the light, the more energy it emits. The light around the brain and the heart, both of which are electrically charged organs, emit a stronger light than organs that don't operate with firing electrons. I find this fact to be simply amazing.

In learning more about God's light, it reminds me of a powerful episode I experienced many years ago. Many people call what encountered a near-death experience. What I know is that it rocked my world.

The experience was so powerful that I was unable to discuss the event for a very long time. I questioned the experience of whether it did happen and if it were real. Since that experience, God has indeed shown me in many different ways that it was indeed something from Him.

I was in my late thirties and went in for what was supposed to be a routine surgery. Two weeks to the date of the operation, I began hemorrhaging severely. By the time the ambulance drove me the 30 minutes to the nearest hospital, I was cold and shaking as my body was going into shock.

After the emergency surgery, I awakened in my darkened hospital room. My most vivid memory was how I still felt exceptionally cold as a result of tremendous blood loss. I became utterly exhausted from shivering as my body continued to convulse.

The room was dark, and I remember seeing my husband in the corner asleep in a chair. The most overwhelming feeling was just wanting to be warm. At that moment, while my eyes were closed, the shivering immediately stopped as the room filled with a fantastic warm light.

I lay there basking in this light's glow. As my thought process caught up with the experience, I thought, *I wonder who turned on the lights in my room?* When I opened my eyes, I couldn't believe the brilliance of how this light completely enveloped every inch of the hospital room.

Even more impressive was how this bright light did not hurt my eyes. I have thought about this experience over the years, yet I have never been able to adequately describe this type of light. No words have ever seemed to do it justice.

The best terms I can use to describe it are pure, brilliant, warm, enveloping, clean. I had never before experienced anything like this light.

There was more, however, than just this brilliant light. At the foot of my bed was an outline of what I knew to be a person or being. I could not see his face because the light was coming from behind him. I use the term him because I knew it was a male form.

Without using a voice as we know it, He said four obvious statements to me that I will never forget. These statements have had a profound effect on my life. Here is what He said:

"You are going to be okay. I have work for you to do."

With my type A personality, I immediately asked, "What work? I'll do whatever you want me to do."

He replied, "In my own time. Now rest, my child."

After He said the last statement, the light was gone. The warmth I felt left, and once again, I became ice cold.

I remember calling out to my husband and saying, "Did you see him? Did you see the man at the foot of my bed?"

He looked at me strangely and shook his head no.

At once, I began to question the entire experience in my mind and started doubting it myself. The event was so incredibly real to me; I know for a fact that it wasn't a dream. The nurses hurriedly entered the room, looking at my charts and readings from the whirring machines and asking if I felt all right.

There was evidence that something had happened because my stats indicated some changes. Not only did my body warm up during that experience, but I felt safe; I was in the presence of someone more significant than myself.

Approximately six months after this incident, we attended a party of a physician friend of ours. I happened to be standing where I could see the front door. When it opened, an elderly gentleman came in using a walker.

At that very moment, I had an intensely strong urge to go and tell this stranger about my "light" experience in the hospital. Now remember, I had never previously seen him and didn't have a clue who he was. I just knew I had an overwhelming need to go and tell him my story.

As I was arguing to myself as to why this was a bad idea and how this man would think I was nuts, I finally found him sitting alone. I asked if I could join him and then said, "Sir, I don't know why, but I need to share a story with you."

I began telling my story, and he immediately grabbed my arm and asked me to stop until he could bring his wife over to also hear it. Tears streamed down his face. I was mortified in thinking I had upset him.

When she joined us, I finished the story, and now all of us were in tears. He then looked right at me and said, "Thank you for sharing this. I was in the hospital about six months ago and was very ill, and I had the same experience you did."

He went on to explain he was the former chief of staff of the local hospital, and as a medical doctor, he had heard these types of stories many times before but always scoffed at them. Now he said, "You have confirmed that my experience was real."

I told him that he too had confirmed my story was real! During those previous six months, I had been questioning my sanity and doubting my experience. This real-life encounter proved for both of us that God had reached us in a very personal way.

I've never seen this man again, yet I am so thankful God placed him at that party for both of us to receive the confirmation of divine intervention. There are no accidents or coincidences when it comes to God. He orchestrates it all and gives us unusual gifts and experiences. To this day, I still marvel at this story.

Including this story in this chapter seemed like the right thing to do as we are focusing on God's radiating light. I was blessed to experience this light and feel honored He allowed me to grasp a glimpse of this radiance. None of us are worthy of this gift of light, yet He gives us all the light which is within Him when we trust in Him.

Let's take a more in-depth look at what science is discovering regarding light. In living organisms, it has been found that living cells emit a light called a biophoton.[2] A biophoton is a tiny emission of light resulting from chemical reactions.

Some organisms, such as jellyfish and certain species of plankton, emit these lights we can see with the naked eye. These animals are called bioluminescent microorganisms.

---

2   TM Srinvasan, "Biophotons as Subtle Energy Carriers," https://www.ncbi.nlm.nih.gov/pmc/articles/PMC5433113/, May 2017.

Another fascinating discovery is with our cells. Scientists have observed a light within our cells, which is so tiny we cannot see it with the naked eye.

Just because we can't see this light, doesn't mean it does not exist. The scientific community has shown great interest in this study of biophotons and what they mean to us. If cells emit light and are altered by the body's chemistry, what ways can this light be altered in terms of diagnosing disease?

One of the most recent and fascinating pieces of information I have come across involves the discovery of a protein within our cells called laminin. This protein is found in the matrix surrounding the inside of a cell. Laminin acts like the glue holding the cell and its parts together.

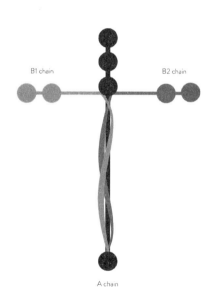

B1 chain

B2 chain

A chain

Without light emitting through the electron microscope, we would have never discovered this tiny little structure. Paul said it very well in Romans 1:22, *"For since the creation of the world God's invisible qualities--his eternal power and divine nature--have been clearly seen, being understood from what has been made, so that people are without excuse."*

Amazingly, the molecular structure of laminin is in the form of a cross. The picture to the right is from the work of Dr. Georgia

Purdom, who holds a Ph.D. in molecular biology and has written some compelling articles on laminin.[3]

There we have it, down to the cellular level. This laminin protein is holding us together, and it is in the shape of a cross! Pastor Louie Giglio spoke about it after he met a molecular biologist who explained laminin to him and showed him how it was in the form of a cross. The verse from Colossians 1:15–17 came alive with new meaning[4]:

> "He is the image of the invisible God, the firstborn over all creation. For by Him, all things were created; things in heaven and on earth, visible and invisible, whether thrones or powers or rulers or authorities; all things were created by Him and for Him. He is before all things, and in Him all things HOLD TOGETHER" (Colossians 1:15–20).

This is a WOW moment that has rocked my world while researching this book. Sure, the naysayers are out there claiming if you look at the actual photograph of laminin, it isn't a perfectly straight cross. Accurate, yet at a molecular level, many of the proteins and structures we observe under a microscope are not all perfectly formed as the drawings of these molecules depict.

There is no doubt; however, the molecular structure of laminin does resemble a cross. At the molecular level is one main vertical base. Two new chains of molecules wrap the main vertical base from the bottom. One filament coils around to one side while the other coils to the other, thus, creating the cross.

---

3   www.answersingenesis.com.

4   Dr. George Purdom," Laminin and the Cross", 2008. https://answersingenesis.org/biology/microbiology/laminin-and-the-cross/.

Another thought regarding the three-strand structure of the umbilical cord as mentioned at the end of Chapter 7 is that laminin, is also comprised of three strands. Unbelievable! My heart jumped out of my chest when I connected this thought. A great designer indeed follows a great design.

Now, if you have stayed with me through the thought process regarding light, we as Christians must be His light. It is our responsibility to shine this light before the world. Our light must not be diminished by anything.

> ""You are the light of the world. A town built on a hill cannot be hidden. Neither do people light a lamp and put it under a bowl. Instead they put it on its stand, and it gives light to everyone in the house. In the same way, let your light shine before others, that they may see your good deeds and glorify your Father in heaven." (Matthew 5:14–16).

It's time for you to get out there and shine your light for the Lord. Be bold and let others see the light radiating from within you. Let it shine; it is the time!

THEOSYNTHESIS®

PART IV

UNLOCKING THE GOD-POTENTIAL IN ALL OF US

CHAPTER 17

EMOTIONAL ENERGY

WE ALL KNOW the powerful effect emotions have on humans. Each of us has experienced the various ranges of emotion from devastation, loss, disappointment, anger, frustration, loneliness, all the way to the opposite end of the emotional spectrum of love, happiness, comfort, pleasure, joy, peace, and utter elation. We simply cannot escape this life without experiencing emotions.

As humans, we often feel like we are on an emotional roller coaster. One day you may experience being on top of the world, and in an instant, you have lost a dear loved one. Life is tenuous and can be very difficult.

Emotions take a toll on us physically as well. Have you ever felt the intense exhaustion after experiencing an emotionally draining situation? It can be all-consuming, leaving you completely raw and frustrated.

Emotions also take a great deal of energy. They emit an energy force that are noticeable by others. Emotions can be felt because of the vibrational qualities they possess.

Maybe you have entered a room full of people and were able to feel the energy within the place. Perhaps you've met someone and instantly felt sadness, anger, or joy radiating from them. You might have picked up on signals from their body language or by a facial expression. Along with the visual cues, you were also feeling the vibrational energy of their emotions.

Our human emotions affect us within every biological level of our bodies. Emotions release hormones and other chemicals directly into our bloodstream that are delivered to every one of our cells. Even down to our microscopic, cellular level, emotions are being communicated.

There are thousands of scientific studies which, have measured the effects of emotional stress on the body.[1] There is no doubt; negative stress can alter and damage healthy cells. The vibrational frequency of negative emotions wreaks havoc on humans, eventually resulting in disease.

The exciting news show that good, positive emotions also emit vibrational frequencies. Positive, emotional frequencies bathe our cells in good chemicals and hormones that promote well-being and health. We also know that these positive emotions strengthen our immune systems.

Do you know those people who are consistently negative, sad, or angry? Most likely, these individuals suffer from all sorts of health issues. Often, people who stay in a continuous state of negative emotions will find that not only do they experience a high rate of physical illnesses, but they also have a propensity to develop mental illnesses.

---

1 Stress Symptoms, https://www.webmd.com/balance/stress-management/ stress-symptoms-effects_of-stress-on-the-body#1, Accessed May, 2020.

I know I can pick up negative emotions or vibes when I am around someone who always seems down. If the feeling is anger or has an evil frequency to it, I am compelled to leave immediately. I have learned to listen to this vibe and to listen to my gut.

Negative, angry emotions cause our bodies to enter into the fight or flight mode. In this manner, our natural, protective method alerts us when we are in danger. And yes, even negative emotions can be hazardous.

Most people, of course, prefer to be around others who emit a joyful heart and spirit and exude good, emotional energy. You may wonder why you are drawn to certain people. The reason is due to the fact being that thoughts and emotions most definitely emit vibrational frequencies.

Have you ever known someone who just always seems to pick themselves up no matter what is happening in their life? There are also those people who always seem to prosper, win, and have success. Why is this?

Having the ability to remain emotionally secure and positive makes a world of difference in our lives. When we truly understand the power of how emotions affect us on every level, we can then begin to work on maintaining the most positive vibrational frequencies we can. And yes, we do have significant control over how we allow different emotions to rule in our lives.

As a believer in Christ, I know I could not have gone through many of the circumstances in my life without leaning on God. As discussed in Chapter 13 on prayer, we learned how prayer affects us on a cellular level. During the times I have gone through the fire, being able to go to a higher power other than myself has been the only thing that helped me from remaining in a negative emotional state.

Of course, there are people who will deny, ignore, or run from negative emotions and situations in their lives. One day, however, they will ultimately find themselves at the end of their power. This is when some reach "the bottom of the barrel."

During our lowest points, finally giving up and allowing God to take over is a good choice. There will always be those people who continue finding their way and their path while others appear to be okay without God. At the end of their lives; however, when standing before God, they will be struck with the reality of much more than just themselves.

Choosing to have zero belief in God must be a sad state of affairs for nonbelievers as they reach the end of their natural lives. If this life on Earth is all there is, I too would be pretty darn messed up and left with no hope. Without God and the promise of eternal life, why even try if this is all there is?

Choosing to deny that God is called *atheism*. "A" means without, and "thesos" refers to God. Those who don't know either way are called *agnostic*. Either way, they have made their choice that God is not important in their lives.

In my encounters with both atheists and agnostics, I find most to be somewhat angry and argumentative with anyone who goes against their beliefs. Approaching the topic of God seems to evoke anger. My desire has always been to have the opportunity to discuss the argument intelligently.

When I meet others who proclaim to be atheists and agnostics, I am not angry they choose not to believe in God. This is their business, and they are on their journey. I do, however, enjoy a good, healthy God debate. I just haven't found a nonbeliever who can also enjoy the debate and doesn't become upset and blow up.

In my opinion, the staunch nonbelievers are entirely repelled due to the God-vibrational frequencies emitted by believers. They feel God's presence, and they don't like it. The darkness simply does not understand the light.

> "Everyone who does evil hates the light, and will not come into the light for fear that their deeds will be exposed. But whoever lives by the truth comes into the light, so that it may be seen plainly that what they have done has been done in the sight of God" (John 3:20).

Evil hates the light! Evildoers don't want their deeds to be exposed. We know this phenomenon is real. And remember, light is power and energy. God's light exposes sin and is the ultimate power source on Earth.

I am sure each of you has encountered a human with no light in their eyes. You can feel this darkness. You are feeling the energy vibrations they emit, and they are authentic and palatable.

You may have also encountered those people who seem to shine from within. The light in their eyes can be seen, and their positive energy can be felt. As John 3:20 above shows us, this light is plainly seen.

I love how God designed the properties of light that always win out over darkness. If you were trapped in a dark cave and lit the tiniest of flames, the light would illuminate and permeate the darkness. However, darkness can never snuff out the light.

The light then absolutely possesses an energetic frequency. Darkness has no frequency.

Therefore, as believers, we are equipped with our own sonar system, if you will, that can detect the lack of vibration or darkness in a person and can also discern evil and danger.

Emotional energy is powerful. Understanding how powerful this energy can be is one of the most important lessons we ever learn as humans. Recognizing the destructive forces of negative energy in our lives can be life-changing. Likewise, embracing positive energy and emotion by going to God for His ultimate energy source will equip you on this exciting and enjoyable journey called life.

Light then absolutely possesses an energetic frequency. Darkness has no frequency. Therefore, as believers, we are equipped with our own sonar system, if you will, that can detect the lack of vibration or darkness in a person and can also discern evil and danger.

As science continues to explore the effects of both positive and negative energies on humans, it will be interesting to follow the findings. Depressed emotional health is an area science is studying. Unfortunately, many of the chemical compounds or medicine used to treat depression have severe side effects.

In Chapter 30, we address the importance of maintaining a healthy chemical balance in your life. Many people who suffer from physiological pain often overmedicate with chemicals that alter their behavior and thoughts. Keeping our bodies as free as possible from chemicals that change our mind and emotions is of significant importance to maintaining stable emotional health.

Certainly, some people are mentally and emotionally ill, and medication may be their only answer. My point is in learning to recognize negative emotions and then how to handle them safely and healthily. Asking God for His help should be the first step. Allowing Him to help you heal the hurts and the emotional pain in life is by far the best method.

In closing this chapter regarding emotional energy, recognizing our emotions are powerful and do affect us at every level is vastly essential. Protecting our emotional health is paramount. Maintaining emotional stability can help make a difference for us on many levels throughout our lives.

During those times in my life when everything appears to be falling apart, I fall in front of Almighty God. He is my Sustainer and supplies me with the much-needed energy when I tap into this source. Connecting to Him provides me with the ability to stabilize my Theosynthetic balance, which helps me maintain stability in both my mental and emotional health.

Perhaps you have never sincerely tried to reach out to God. Maybe it's time to stop trying to solve your problems. You might find the energy source God can provide is something you have been searching for all of your life.

CHAPTER 18

CREATIVE ENERGY

I AM EXCITED to explore this chapter regarding creative energy. Discovering creative energy has been a significant revelation in my own life. Join me as we delve into this fascinating topic.

Do you find some people appear to possess natural creativity? It seems everything they touch turns into something surprising or unique. What is it then about this thing we call creativity?

First of all, understanding that God, the Intelligent Designer, created us can help us grasp what creativity means. We are not creative beings on our own. Because the ultimate creative Force formed us, we too can be able to co-create with God.

This thought may seem a bit crazy, but stick with me, and I believe you will understand what I mean to be creative. I think once you genuinely do comprehend it, you might just discover your amazing abilities that otherwise might have been hidden or suppressed.

I hear people all of the time saying things like, "I don't have a creative bone in my body." Let me tell you, if you believe this statement to be accurate, you have been fed a pack of lies! It is *not* true in the least. As created beings in God's own image, each of us possesses creative abilities. That's right; every one of us can be creative in some unique way.

Why then, if we possess creative abilities, are there so many people who just go through the motions in their lives? They appear to lack ideas, motivation, or any talent. The answer lies in the fact that many people believe they don't have any creative abilities.

If you have ever observed a child playing, you've witnessed the innocence with which they freely play. When a child is in a safe environment, they will play, discover, and create naturally. Games of make-believe and free-dance movements are natural and carefree. Notice the key phrase here is "being in a safe environment."

When then, did we stop playing, creating, and imagining in our lives? Many of us can't even remember when we ceased having a playful, fun, and free attitude. We have become so driven in our careers and lives that we don't leave any time to play, create, and to explore.

Creativity is an energetic force in its own right. This topic is exciting to me because of the way Theosynthesis came into existence. Because I stayed tapped into God and was open to hearing from Him, He allowed me to co-create with Him. This concept is a gamechanger, people!

Understanding every human being possesses an incredible ability to co-create with God is mind-blowing. Why then, do so many people believe they are not creative or perhaps choose to ignore the hidden talents within them? Deep down, don't we all desire to create, discover, imagine, and to play?

As I discussed previously, children naturally play and create when they feel safe and loved. However, when children or adults are placed in situations where they no longer feel safe, most likely, they will shut down. When this happens, our creative abilities go underground.

Sadly, many people are told they are not worthy, or maybe they were shunned for their ideas. When we experience rejection in any form, which injures our heart and emotions, many will retreat and never again revive their creative outlet—what an unfortunate thing.

God desires each one of us to use our God-given gifts and talents. When we tap into His energy source, these talents can be manifested and put to good use. Because God made all of us with creative abilities, even those who deny Him still possess these talents.

Of course, not all talented and creative people are believers in God. They deem they naturally possess these creative ideas and skills on their own. Some will be very successful, while many will not.

Let's take a look at Hollywood. I love a good movie or concert and have nothing against ultra-creative people. My point with Hollywood remains that we all know many sad instances of super-creative people who were depressed, lonely, and on a path of self-destruction.

You can certainly have all of the money in the world, be extraordinarily talented, and yet still not be satisfied with life in general. The bottom line is this—without someone more significant than yourself in life, the God-gap is experienced in some form. Remember, God created us down to our DNA to know and seek Him. If we ignore or deny Him, we will be out of balance.

In my own life, when I stay deeply connected with God, He puts thoughts and ideas in my head like never before. When I experience those brain-dead moments where I don't feel creative, I know I need just to stop and spend time in His presence. I need to recharge and plugin with the God of the universe.

The God of the universe desires to co-create with you and me. This was a mind-blowing concept to me when I first recognized it. Doesn't it make sense, however? Our amazing God honestly does want us to be in tune with Him so that we can tap into the abundance of energy He has available to each of us.

If you are one of those people who have not yet discovered what your talents and skills are, or perhaps you believe you don't possess any creativity, I ask you to stop right now and go to God. Ask Him to show you, guide you, and encourage you. When you go to the right energy source, you will be amazed by what God has to show you.

Everyone is gifted. God doesn't make mistakes. Believing this and going to Him reverently and openly is your first step in discovering what your gifts are.

From my own experience, when I get into a creative mode, whether writing, decorating, or working on a new concept, I am completely energized. Why is this? Because creativity has its own energy.

During the time I am writing this book while taking breaks, I cannot wait to get back to my computer to continue to write. I am excited and energized. Creativity radiates out of you and is felt.

Again, just observe a child at play. You can feel their energy as they are free to create and make-believe. This gift of creative energy is no different for adults, if only we would allow ourselves to engage in this creative force.

Imagine how different our world would be if everyone truly recognized that they too had the power to create, explore, imagine, and then actually acted on these gifts? All of us can do things we never thought possible. If only we could simply believe in the untapped gifts of creativity just waiting to burst through, what possibilities might there be?

What is it you have always dreamt of doing? Have you been told your ideas were crazy and unachievable? Maybe you have falsely told yourself you have nothing to contribute to this world.

Imagine how different our world would be if everyone truly recognized that they too had the power to create, explore, imagine, and then actually acted on these gifts?

Perhaps someone told you these untruths, and you believed them.

Nothing could be farther from the truth. Why don't you stop buying into these lies and see how your life could be different if you began to sincerely believe in your dreams? Who knows what amazing achievements will be achieved when you do?

I never thought I would be a published author. I've always loved writing poetry, creating curricula, and speaking in front of groups. It wasn't until I finally quit listening to the nay-naysayers (mainly myself) and began to tap into my true God-given abilities did I begin to embrace this aspect of my life.

When the idea of Theosynthesis came to me, I could have dismissed it as ridiculous. I have wrestled with the entire concept many times. I've asked why God would choose me to bring this topic to light? At the time of the revelation of Theosynthesis, I did not possess a Ph.D. nor was I a theologian. I've had to come to terms that God *did* choose me; therefore, I must be obedient to bring it to life.

I pray that each person reading this book will take a moment to understand what talents lie within them that could change the world. You have God-enabled potential to do whatever it is you yearn to do. Why not give it a try?

As you unleash the creative forces within you, brace yourself for some incredible results. Allowing yourself to explore your hidden talents will provide you with an energy that will flow through your body, awakening those slumbering ideas. The creative energy force within you will fuel you like nothing else.

As you tap into God's rich energy source, He will delight in watching you soar. This energy is just like the bubbling lava energy lurking beneath the earth's surface. We know it is there, and when it is released, BAM! Get ready and enjoy this truth.

Grab a journal and write down all of the desires of your heart. No matter how crazy they might appear, put them down on paper. Next, pray over these ideas. Ask God to reveal clearly to you what He requires of you and how to do it.

Finally, get busy! Don't make excuses, and don't waste the talents God has given you. If He has gifted you with something, He has entrusted it to you. Telling God no or telling Him you can't or won't is not a wise thing to do.

How will you answer the call God is asking of you? What proactive steps must you do today to get you out of your comfort zone and into God's chosen path for your life? Never has there been a better time than right now!

CHAPTER 19

CO-CREATING WITH THE CREATOR

ISN'T IT EXCITING to understand we all possess a creative force within us? Once we embrace this concept and begin allowing ourselves to believe it and then act upon it, we can then begin to co-create with our Creator. This truth, my friends, is a game-changer!

When you feel you are contributing your talents in this life, you feel connected, needed, and essential. God desires for each of us use the skills He gave us. He created each of us with our own unique and specific gifts.

Recognizing these gifts are from God is the point where He can begin to use them. Too many times, creative people mistakenly believe their talents are their own. However, when we humbly give credit to the One who enabled these gifts within us, He will bless your life more richly than you can imagine.

The crux of the entire idea of Theosynthesis came about because I was in tune with God. As I trusted Him by writing and putting myself out there, He has continued allowing me to then co-create with Him. As I remain connected to Him, ideas pour out of me.

A few years ago while attending a John Maxwell event with thousands of other like-minded, highly creative people, the room truly felt electric. Three thousand individuals, all co-creating and being together in the same place, emitted mind-boggling energy.

If you have never experienced being in a room with thousands of creative, energetic people, make sure you find the time to experience this. Not only will this type of event encourage you, but you will also then understand what I am talking about with all of this energy talk. You will leave the event more energized and ready to take on just about anything.

In the last chapter, we discussed the untold amounts of creativity that people possess. Why do so many fail to ever explore this? Somewhere along the way in their life, they began to falsely believe they have nothing to contribute. One discouraging word, experience, or perhaps too many bumps in their road, caused them to stop believing in themselves.

Fear is what happens to the majority of people who never move forward with a dream or an idea. Plain and simple, fear of failure or embarrassment prevents most people from attempting a new approach or plan.

Fear is what happens to the majority of people who never move forward with a dream or an idea. Plain and simple, fear of failure or embarrassment prevents most people from attempting a new idea or plan.

Why do we fear to try new things? First of all, it is essential to understand fear. According to the dictionary, fear is simply an unpleasant emotion caused by the belief that someone or something is dangerous, likely to cause pain, or is a threat. Fear of failure for many is more frightening than anything else they may encounter.

Let's take a look at what failure is and what it isn't. Unfortunately, most people believe that failure is always a negative thing. This is not true at all. I firmly believe failure is the one thing that can propel us to reach our desired goal or that seemingly elusive dream.

When we learn to walk, we spend a lot of time falling. We get hurt and bump our heads. Does this mean all of those falls were failures? Not at all! Without those falls, we wouldn't have learned the basic movements and patterns that would eventually make us successful to finally walk.

Our brains are wired to learn. Each time we hear, see, or read something new, the brain imprints this and sends messages to those areas of our body that need the information. The skills required for walking teaches a toddler what works and what doesn't as they teeter and totter their way to successfully walking. The learned responses from what didn't work enabled them to eventually walk.

Additionally, as we continue to learn, muscles are strengthened, neurons connect, and the brain-body connection occurs. Without practice, these skills are not mastered. Repeated patterns develop the necessary skills needed in our lives.

This fact is actual for every learned skill in our lives. For many, when they don't achieve instant success at something new, they prematurely give up. How sad and unfortunate that before discovering eventual success or progression, they allowed what they perceived to attempt as a failure.

There are many incidences of individuals who kept on trying and attempting something despite numerous failures. They overcame all of the odds and the adverse reactions from other people.

These are people who are just like you and me who experienced failure, yet they never stopped trying and believing. Let's take a look at a few of these people.

Henry Ford was a man who found he had to try many times before he finally found success in the car industry. He attempted several businesses and was flat broke before he finally succeeded in what we now know as the Ford Motor Company. Because he didn't give up, our world was forever changed.

Thomas Edison was told when he was young that he was not smart. What if he believed this? His most noteworthy achievement, among many others, was the light bulb. Yet it took over 1,000 failed attempts before he finally discovered the design that worked. His perseverance enabled him to "see the light."

Elvis Presley was once told he would never amount to anything in the music industry. Had he believed this, we might not enjoy his unique musical sound and talent. Thankfully, he too continued thinking he did have something to offer the world.

And let's look at Michael Jordan. We know him as one of the greatest athletes of all time. However, did you know he was cut from his basketball team in high school? This event could have been a devastating setback for him, yet he pushed on and proved he was a force to be reckoned with in his sport. How many missed baskets did he throw in practices and games? A lot!

I think you can see my point. Failures are not failures unless we believe them to be so. Learning does not take place without experiencing mistakes. Success comes when we continue to learn, and we strive to move forward even when the results are not what we wanted them to be.

What is it you desire to do right now? Do you feel too old? Unprepared? Not talented enough? Remember, those are not the thoughts of God. He wishes very much to co-create with you and me.

The bottom line is that we must stay tuned in to God's energy source. You have an untapped, unbelievable amount of creative energy within yourself. Stop trying to utilize this creative energy without first connecting to the only real energy source.

God is ready to co-create with you right now. You've always possessed the ability to tap into this energy. Now is the time. The next chapter will focus on how to align with God to tap into His power and your own. Knowing His will for our lives is an important key.

Here are a few scripture verses to encourage us when we fall short: In Jeremiah 8:4, Jeremiah said this to the people of Judah:

"This is what the Lord says: 'You know if a man falls down, he gets up again. And if a man goes the wrong way, he turns around and comes back.'"

"The righteous may fall seven times but still get up, but the wicked will stumble into trouble" (1 Peter 1:5).

"The LORD is the one who is going ahead of you. He will be with you. He won't abandon you or leave you. So don't be afraid or terrified" (Deuteronomy 31:8).

"The steps of a good man are ordered by the Lord: and he delighteth in his way. Though he fall, he shall not be utterly cast down: for the Lord upholdeth him with his hand" (Psalm 37:23–24).

Isn't it evident that God is invested in our lives, cares deeply for us, and desires for us to learn from every life situation? As mentioned earlier, He wants us to use our God-given talents. Are you ready to get busy seeking them out and utilizing them?

If you have attempted to do something and failed, reassess, revisit, and reinvent a new or different way to succeed. Ask God to help you and show you what He desires from you. Often, we attempt our human-led ideas before humbly going before Him to seek His blessing and advice.

The main takeaway from this chapter is in knowing we are each uniquely designed to co-create with God. I find this concept very encouraging and exciting. What is your dream? Now is the time to discover those goals.

CHAPTER 20

CREATED TO WORK

HAVING OBSERVED how our Creator desires to create with us, let's now take a look into the important concept of work. God created man to work. We were not made to simply sit around all day being nonproductive.

Many consider work to be a negative thing. Perhaps the reason they don't enjoy it could be because they don't know the gifts and talents they possess. From my own experiences, when I am doing something I am passionate about, it never feels like work.

Work can be defined is in many ways. The Merriam-Webster Dictionary defines work as an activity involving mental or physical effort done to achieve a purpose or result.

A keyword here is effort. For work to be achieved, one

Understanding we were created with a purpose, discovering this purpose and moving forward with it is crucial. Choosing to live a life with a focused plan rather than simply feeding off of what others do, is not how God intended us to live.

must put forth an effort. The second part of this definition is also important. An action must be part of the equation to achieve a purpose or result.

This is where the rubber meets the road—purpose and results. If you are simply toiling away at something without knowing your purpose or having an outcome for your results, you most likely are merely going through the motions. How many people do you know who despise their work and day in and day out, mindlessly go through a routine?

Work as God designed it does have a purpose and indeed require results. Let's take a walk back into the Garden of Eden.

"By the seventh day, God had finished the work He had been doing; so on the seventh day, He rested from all His work" (Genesis 2:2)

Right away in the Scriptures we see the first mention of the word "work." God's amazing creation of the world and man were His work. God isn't idle, and He is always at work. Now, let's take a look at the first created man, Adam.

"The Lord God took the man and put him in the Garden of Eden to work it and take care of it" (Genesis 2:15).

God created the first man and gave him a job to do. Adam was not merely created to lounge all day in the garden and be idle. He was required to put effort into his job and to take pride in the task. Nowhere is it mentioned that Adam or any man is to be lazy.

Understanding we were created with a purpose, discovering this purpose, and moving forward with it is crucial. Choosing to live a life with a focused plan rather than merely feeding off what others do is not how God intended us to live. All of us at some level understand this simple concept.

Sadly, in our world today, many people believe they shouldn't have to work or are above working. Some have been oppressed by doing unfair work for others. Then others go to work doing something they dislike.

God did not intend work to be this way for us. Within each one of us, however, lies the ability to work, create, inspire, or teach. And guess what? All of these actions require effort, planning, learning, and most importantly, a positive attitude toward their work.

Today we see many people in society who simply want a handout. They claim a desire to escape poverty or oppression, yet they hold out their hand to be fed by others. However, this is what ultimately keeps people in poverty.

We know from history that some government systems are designed to even out the playing field in a socialistic manner. Historically, all have failed. By keeping people in a constant state of need has never been God's design for humanity. Contributing to the world through efforts of your work is what provides us with purpose and fulfillment in life.

Our bodies and minds are not designed to be lazy. The human body is made up of strong muscles, bones, and ligaments. These structures allow us to move. God created us to move! We were not made to be sedentary. Additionally, our brain is designed to think. The brain also has more cognitive capacity than we can ever tap into during our lifetime.

When we neglect our brain by filling it with unnecessary things or with smut and trash, it will also become mush. Take care of what you allow into your mind. Protect the images you view. This fantastic structure of the brain is like a computer—Fill it with junk, and it will produce garbage.

What happens when we neglect our physical body or our minds? That's right; they go to mush. We must challenge the body and the mind with a good work ethic daily. We will expand this concept in the next few chapters.

In keeping with our topic of Theosynthesis, understanding we were made to work is vitally important. If you have yet to find the work you are passionate about, then get out there and find it. What a difference you'll have in the concept of work when you engage in something that resonates deeply within your soul.

If you feel out of balance in the area of your work, go to your ultimate source—God. Aligning with Him is the only way to tap into the fantastic source of creativity and energy. He supplies this to everyone who desires to connect with Him.

Are you ready to collaborate with the Almighty? Imagine the possibilities available to you when you trust God, who desires to collaborate with you. This concept alone will change the way you view your work.

What a privilege it is to have the opportunity to work directly with God! We can either choose to embrace this gift or reject it. His door is open to us; all that is required is the right attitude to go before Him willingly.

Your path in life and the choices you make each day are up to you. Because you are created as a being of free will, simple decisions, such as what to eat, to choices of beliefs and faith are yours alone to make.

Deciding to connect with God is a choice. Choosing to tap into His power and strength will make a significant difference in your life.

Imagine the difference if you truly took the time to fill yourself with this power He provides?

Choose today to reach out to God with your needs, your desires, and your ideas. Allow Him to guide you with the decisions you need to make. Ask Him to give you a passion for your work and to help you identify what it is that creates a fire within you.

I know that any kind of work can be meaningful. We have all read or seen the stories of people in jobs they may deem as being beneath them. Yet now and then, we see an example of someone who has an attitude of gratitude in everything they do. They do not feel sorry for themselves, and they simply do their work with a happy and grateful heart.

The verse from Colossians 3:23–24 says, *"Whatever you do, work heartily, as for the Lord, and not for men, knowing that from the Lord you will receive the inheritance as your reward. You are serving the Lord Christ."*

There it is, "whatever" you do! In all things! We are to work wholeheartedly as for the Lord. Do you see this? This Scripture is teaching us about having the right attitude toward our work.

Who then can help us get this right attitude? God is the only One who can truly guide us in being able to possess this attitude of gratitude. Those who worship themselves will eventually find an emptiness at the end of the day.

If you find yourself in a rut regarding your work, take a moment to reflect on why you are in this line of work? What, if anything else, would you genuinely want to do? How can you move forward into a job or position that is meaningful to you?

Finding your passion and then developing the skills that will enable you to work in that passion are quite rewarding. Many, including myself, have experienced several different career paths. There is no shame in this, and it merely indicates you are a seeker.

To do the work you desire, you will most likely need specific knowledge and skills. Many people try and skip the necessary steps for preparation. There are no shortcuts when you are developing the skills to do a job well.

Additionally, doing any job with the utmost attention to detail is crucial. Whatever vocation you have been placed in, completing the work in the best manner possible is fundamental. Choosing to cut corners is not the way you were designed to work.

As stated earlier, ask God to help you find your passion regarding work. Maybe it is right under your nose, and you just haven't looked in the right direction. Regardless, God wants you working and desires you to perform your work duties with zeal. Perhaps what is missing is simply having the right attitude.

Imagine a world where everyone took this biblical principle to heart. Might we then find joy in all things? Discover pleasant people? Experience those people who are working for a bigger picture other than themselves!

Because we live in a fallen and sin-filled world where there is a free choice, we shall never see this type of peace on Earth. However, that, does not mean you and I can't make a difference with how we choose to work. Thankfully, there are many people out there who do work as unto the Lord.

As we continue our discussion on Theosynthesis, doesn't it make sense that when fully connected to God, our work ethic is reflected as well? When the Son light gives us power, we will genuinely radiate Him through all that we do. Working as unto the Lord changes everything.

Are you experiencing your work with passion and purpose? An excellent book and resource, *The Purpose Driven Life* by Pastor Rick Warren, discusses in great detail how to live a life of purpose. If you can't seem to find your purpose, perhaps this book will guide you in the right direction.

CHAPTER 21

ALIGNING WITH GOD

AS WE continue unveiling the concept of Theosynthesis, the word "alignment" keeps coming to mind. To align is to place things in a straight line or in a proper order. It can also mean working together with someone to form an alliance or agreement.

Is it possible to believe in God yet not align with Him? The answer is yes, and sadly for many, this is the exactly the case. There are people who say, "Yes, there is a God, yet I don't really feel the need to pray to Him, worship Him, or read the Bible." With this type of example, these people would not be aligned with God. There is an absence of an alliance or an agreement.

Often, people simply go through life believing in God yet never arrive at a place of aligning with Him. Typically, this type of relationship is one-sided. God is there for them when *they* need Him, but there is no effort on their part to spend any time or thought with Him when they don't see the need for Him.

Why then, is it important to be aligned with God? Hopefully, this is being confirmed for you as you continue reading this book. In order to be whole or complete, we must have the God connection.

Our anchor and our tether to align with God is what provides the balance in our lives.

When my car is out of alignment, it ceases to function properly. If I don't take the car into the shop to have it corrected, eventually it will stop working altogether. If my back or spine is out of alignment, I experience a great deal of discomfort and must seek someone who can help me become realigned.

It makes sense then, being in alignment with God is an essential part of life. This means much more than simply believing in Him. As we spend time with Him in His Word, we come to know Him at a deeper level, and our minds become more aligned with His mind.

Oswald Chambers wrote, "All Christians have the spirit of Christ, but not all Christians have the mind of Christ."

In Chambers's writings in the "Utmost of His Highest," he writes: "Is your mind stayed on God or is it starved? Starvation of the mind, caused by neglect, is one of the chief sources of exhaustion and weakness in a servant's life. If you have never used your mind to place yourself before God, begin to do it now. There is no reason to wait for God to come to you. You must turn your thoughts and your eyes away from the face of idols and look to Him and be saved."

> "If you have never used your mind to place yourself before God, begin to do it now. There is no reason to wait for God to come to you. You must turn your thoughts and your eyes away from the face of idols and look to Him and be saved."
>
> OSWALD CHAMBERS, *UTMOST OF HIS HIGHEST*

In order to be aligned with God, we must align our thinking and our minds to reflect Him. Here are some key Scripture verses on this topic:

*"Love the Lord your God with all of your heart and with all of your soul and with all of your **mind**" (Matthew 22:37).*

*"Love the Lord your God with all of your heart, with all of your soul and with all of your **mind** and with all of your strength" (Mark 12:30).*

*"Love the Lord your God with all your heart and with all of your soul and with all of your strength and will all of your **mind**" (Luke 10:27).*

*"And He who searches our hearts knows the **mind** of the Spirit, because the Spirit intercedes for the saints in accordance with God's will" (Romans 8:27).*

*"Do not conform any longer to the pattern of this world, be ye transformed by the renewing of your **mind**" (Romans 12:2).*

*"I appeal to your, brother, in the name of our Lord Jesus Christ, that all of you agree with one another so that there may be no divisions among you and that you may be perfectly united in **mind** and thought" (1 Corinthians 1:10).*

*"For who has known the **mind** of the Lord that He may instruct him? But we have the mind of Christ" (1 Corinthians 2:16).*

*"Who has understood the **mind** of the Lord?" (Isaiah 40:13).*

*"To be made new in the attitude of your **minds**; and to put on the new self, created to be like God in true righteousness and holiness" (Ephesians 4:23–24).*

*"'I will put the covenant I will make with the house of Israel after that time, declares the Lord. I will put My laws in their **minds** and write them on their hearts'" (Hebrews 8:10).*

*"This calls for a **mind** with wisdom" (Revelation 17:9).*

Isn't it evident that God created man with a mind to be used for His purposes? Subsequently, He also created us to have the choice of free will. We were not created as puppets for a grand puppeteer. God gives us all the choice whether or not to align our minds and life with Him.

God calls us to Love Him with *all* of our minds. He doesn't just say we are to love and adore Him; He is telling us we need to use our minds wholeheartedly for God's kingdom. How then do we accomplish this?

In order to align with something, you must first have an understanding regarding the alignment. Knowing God's Word is a huge step in becoming aligned with His Word and then ultimately, to be in line with Him. Therefore, your mind must have an open heart in order to know what He has to teach you.

During my years of teaching biology, one of the most upsetting experiences was watching a student in class who did not apply their natural gift of intelligence. Watching them waste their mind was difficult to accept. I can only imagine God's broken heart when He too watches us waste the beautiful mind He gave to each one of us.

How much of my mind have I wasted on things that really didn't mean anything? It pains me to think about it. I know throughout my life, there have been more times than I would like to remember where I wasted precious mind time on what others thought about me, watching junk on TV, or by simply being lazy.

Staying in God's Word and learning what He has to say is essential in aligning ourselves with the Almighty. What are you focused on right now that is wasting your precious time and energy and thoughts? Turn to Him, and seek His will this very moment.

In the Romans 8:27, we're told, "*And He who searches our hearts knows the mind of the Spirit, because the Spirit intercedes for the saints in accordance with God's will.*" This verse clearly shows us that the *mind* of the Holy Spirit is also at work *in* us. This goes back to the Greek term "rhema," the unspoken Word. When we align with Christ, His Spirit is interceding, guiding, and directing us. We are never, ever on our own.

Another great verse to help us understand this point comes from Romans 12:2: "*Do not conform any longer to the pattern of this world, be ye transformed by the renewing of your mind.*" We are encouraged to *renew* our mind. Renewal refers to a transformation, which means to completely change.

To completely change our minds requires a metamorphosis of the heart and occurs as we walk with Christ daily. In order to renew our mind, we can no longer think as we used to prior to becoming a Christian. This is why the verse says, "Do not *conform* any longer to the pattern of this world."

If you wish to align with God, you must rewire your mind. Your actions and words must be different as you conform to your new Christian life. There must be an inward as well as an outward transformation. Without a renewing of the mind, you will be trapped in your former ways of thinking.

Let's pause for a moment and discuss the brain and what an incredible organ it is. The mind/brain is an amazingly, complicated structure.[1] Doctors and scientists still don't fully understand this intricate organ. Science only understands a fraction of what the mind is truly capable of. This fascinating structure that fires from electrical neurons is one of the most awe-inspiring structures in our entire body.

Just like the whole body itself, when we neglect the mind due to laziness and exposure to toxic chemicals, then deterioration, disease, and disharmony will eventually occur. The mind, just as the muscles of our body, must be used, challenged, enriched, educated, and protected. As we fill our minds with the things of God, we align with His ways and are able to continue developing the mind of Christ within ourselves.

In 1 Corinthians verse 1:10, it says, "*I appeal to you, brothers and sisters, in the name of our Lord Jesus Christ, that all of you agree with one another so that there may be no divisions among you and that you may be perfectly united in mind and thought.*"

It is clear as believers that we must be united together in our minds in order to do the work for the kingdom. Sadly, many churches and Christian organizations are missing this principle entirely. Imagine what we could do as Christians if we faithfully and earnestly worked in *union* with one another for Him?

The Ephesians verse 4:23 "*To be made new in the attitude of your minds; and to put on the new self, created to be like God in true righteousness*

---

1   https://www.nationalgeographic.com/news/2018/03/why-the-brain-body-connection-is-more-important-than-we-think/.

and holiness," shows us that we even gain a new attitude when we are made new as a Christian. The key word here is "attitude." You can have all the academic knowledge of the Bible and of God, yet if you don't possess the right attitude, then you will lose the entire point of having a mind like that of Christ's.

An attitude can be expressed either in a negative or positive manner. Each of us individually is responsible for our own attitude. The attitude we display to the world is completely within our own control. As Christians, we must constantly strive for having an attitude aligned with Christ.

These behaviors and attitudes are clearly seen in Galatians 5:22–34:

> "*But the fruit of the Spirit is love, joy, peace, forbearance, kindness, goodness, faithfulness, gentleness and self-control.*"

As Christians, these nine attitudes or behaviors must be attributes we continue to master as we conform our lives with Christ and to His ways. I'm not saying this is an easy task; rather, we must constantly work on developing these behaviors as we become sanctified in our daily walk with Him.

Finally, we can clearly see in Revelation 17:9 that "*This calls for a mind with wisdom.*" Therefore, we must endeavor to possess a mind of wisdom. Other words used to describe wisdom are insight, perception, and discernment.

Another way of looking at wisdom is that it is not simply having knowledge for the sake of knowledge. Wisdom goes much deeper as it allows us to make better judgement calls and sound decisions. This maturity comes from experience and, of course, aligning ourselves with God.

If you earnestly desire to be aligned with God, you must begin with an open mind willing to hear Him, to know Him, and to follow His laws. This process is a lifelong challenge and one we must rely on the Holy Spirit to help us navigate. The journey begins with you inviting God as your aligned leader. Are you ready to take the first steps?

CHAPTER 22

COLLABORATING WITH GOD

AS I HAVE been humbly collaborating with God while writing this book, I've allowed myself to receive what He has been pouring into me. It has been quite a fantastic experience. Many times, I have asked myself, "What on Earth am I doing?"; "Will people understand this topic of Theosynthesis?"; "Does this work even matter?"

Collaboration is the action of working with someone to produce or create something. Collaborating with God, then, is by being a willing partner with Him. We must participate with Him, which requires actions.

I have come to realize that yes, God put *me* in charge of working with Him on this project. He *chose* me, and I accepted the assignment. Time and again, however, when doubt would creep into my conscience and shake my confidence, He would gently guide me into this work and provide me with the time, energy, and the research to complete it.

Without a shadow of a doubt, I could not have done this on my own. This entire work is God's alone, of which He allowed me to be a part. "Why me" is the question I often ask myself many times? The answer I continue to hear is "Why not me?" As I wrestle with the responsibility of this project, He continues to place people into my life who have encouraged and supported me.

The times I became distracted or wanted to give up, my loving Father would gently pick me up and show me in so many beautiful ways how He wanted me to complete this work. I give Him all of the glory.

During this time of collaborating with God, He will ask more of you than you believe you can do on your own. There is no way Theosynthesis just popped into my head magically. He ordained it, and I have obediently stepped out in faith.

Pondering these types of thoughts, I wondered how many others out there have been gifted by an idea or notion and said, "Me? No way!" I am sure that if I looked back over my life, I have missed numerous other God opportunities because I said no or didn't believe I could do something.

What has become crystal clear in this adventure of writing this book is knowing He ordained *me* to do the work. Again, this is a very humbling realization, and it has been a tremendous responsibility. I keep going back to Colossians 3:23–24: "*Whatever you do, work at it with all your heart, as working for the Lord, not for human masters, since you know that you will receive an inheritance from the Lord as a reward. It is the Lord Christ you are serving.*"

This verse spurred me on when the doubting thoughts emerged. I am not doing this project for myself. I am doing it for the Lord. Therefore, I began working on this book with complete faith and trust in Him to lead and guide me every step of the way—what an incredible experience it has been.

As I prayed about this chapter regarding collaboration with God, my own experience was my best illustration. When I would get into a slump, I depended on Him to show me the way. Rest assured that had I tried to do this on my own, I would have never, ever completed the book.

Additionally, I have learned to discern hearing the voice of God. Knowing the character of God, I had to recognize the doubts were not from Him. Those doubts come from the one who desires us to feel weak, hopeless, scared, and unqualified. Satan wants us to hear his whispers of uncertainty to derail us from our God-given tasks.

I choose to place my faith and trust in God and to call those doubts about what they are—lies! Satan is subtle in his cunning ways. Remaining close to God helps me recognize what is right and what is not valid.

Hopefully, this illustration will help you as you prayerfully navigate a task God has asked of you. Please understand, I am not insinuating that every job God has us do for Him is a huge one. Even things we might think are small in scale can have a significant impact for the kingdom.

This chapter then is to serve as my encouragement to you. What task or job have you been doubting you are capable of doing? Have you felt the stirrings within your heart that there is something bigger than yourself?

Some of the ways I can encourage you are simply the things I have done that have assisted me along in my journey. I hope these tips will help you. I pray you will go before our Father and ask Him to show you the way He has lined out for you.

GUIDELINES TO COLLABORATE WITH GOD

1. **JOURNAL YOUR THOUGHTS.** When you have an idea or thought, no matter how strange it sounds to you, please put it on paper. You don't have to do anything with it right that minute. Writing it down, however, will help you when you are ready to go back and put it in front of God.

2. **PRAY FOR GUIDANCE.** If God is nudging you to do something, He will indeed show you precisely what you need to do. Spending time in prayer and awaiting Him to guide you is by far the best method. Boldly ask Him to show you what and how you need to begin whatever it is He is asking of you.

3. **SEEK GUIDANCE FROM FELLOW BELIEVERS.** If God is asking you to do something, He will place the people in your life to assist you. To do this begins by surrounding yourself with key people you know you can trust, who will encourage you and will hold you accountable.

4. **MAKE A PLAN.** I could not have completed this book without a well-thought-out plan. This step, of course, took time and organization. Outlining your thoughts into bite-sized nuggets is the first step in getting to an end-result. The skeleton outline of a plan can help you visualize the big picture. Ask God to show you precisely what steps you will need to do to complete the task.

5. **EXECUTE.** Many great plans never come to fruition due to a failure to get the project off the ground. Also, many people give up before they see their dream come to life. Perhaps you have failed to launch your ideas, your thoughts, and your goals. If so, go back to step one above and get busy. None of us has been placed on this earth to watch it all go right past us. God has given each of His children gifts and talents. What excuses are you giving Him that is preventing you from moving forward?

Today is your day to begin a new way of thinking. Is this the day you will remember as the time you decided to forge ahead with what seemed to be a far-fetched dream? God has a plan for you and desires for you to align your ideas with His. Now is the time. Why not just get going and go for it?

CHAPTER 23

DAILY CHOICES

NOW THAT YOU have some specific steps to begin walking in obedience with God, you have no excuse but to do something with this new knowledge. You do have choices. Your free will provides you with the opportunity to say either yes or no when it comes to those choices.

When God showed up in my life and said, "Theosynthesis," I could have quickly scoffed it off as some crazy idea. I could have never written the word down, yet I did. I had a choice, and I chose to move ahead with the plan even though it seemed crazy at first.

Indecision, however, is not an option. You don't get to sit on the fence with God. He is quite clear about this. How many of us, though, are just stuck and paralyzed in our walk with God?

Let's look at a few Scriptures regarding indecisiveness:

"If any of you lacks wisdom, he should ask God, who gives generously to all without finding fault, and it will be given to him. But when he asks, he must believe and not doubt, because he who doubts is like a wave of the sea, blown and tossed by the

wind. That man should not think he will receive anything from the Lord; he is a double-minded man, unstable in all he does" (James 1:5–8).

This verse hits home on many points. Ask it of God, believe it, and stop doubting Him. He says in the above verse, *"He is double-minded and unstable."* He is referring to those who won't make a decision one way or another. Woah, God is quite clear regarding His thoughts on this topic.

I'm not sure about you, but I get frustrated very easily by people who cannot make up their minds. Sure, some situations and circumstances are challenging, yet at some point, an eventual decision of some kind must be made. Sticking your head in the sand or looking the other direction is never the answer.

God is also particular about His people being indecisive. In 1 Kings 18:21, *"Elijah went before the people and said, how long will you waver between two opinions? If the Lord is God, follow Him; but if Baal is God, follow him."*

Jesus is quite graphic in His words regarding this topic. Revelation 3:15–16 says, *"I know your deeds, that you are neither cold nor hot. I wish you were either one or the other. So, because you are lukewarm, neither hot nor cold, I am about to spit you out of my mouth."*

Yes, I would say this verse very clearly demonstrates how God looks upon indecision. He would rather vomit you out of His mouth than deal with you. Yikes. It is impossible to please everyone. Attempting to please everyone will get you in trouble most of the time.

God asks us to stick with Him, listen to Him, and to follow Him.

"For the Son of God, Jesus Christ, whom we preached among you, Silva'nus and Timothy and I, was not Yes and No, but in Him, it is always Yes. For all the promises of God find their Yes in him. That is why we utter the Amen through him, to the glory of God" (2 Corinthians 1:19–20).

Trying to remain popular or neutral is not what the Lord wants from any of us. He desires for us to stand firm for His kingdom and to stand up for what is right. Therefore, the apostle Paul said, *"Finally, be strong in the Lordand in his mighty power."* (Ephesians 6:10).

Putting on armor very clearly suggests that things in this world will not always be easy. Living a Christian life doesn't mean it will be all candy and roses from here on out. Jesus knew our walk with Him would be challenging. He knew we would face tough decisions.

Jesus was also faced with tough decisions. He was tempted during His time on this earth. In Mark 4:3, Jesus was tempted by the devil after being out in the desert for 40 days. Satan said to Jesus, *"If you are the Son of God, tell these stones to become bread."*

For us to ever think we are somehow immune from pain and tough experiences in life simply because we are Christians is not what the Bible teaches. During my years on this earth, I see firsthand how it is becoming more and more challenging for Christians in the United States and abroad. Attacks are coming from all sides.

Our faith is being challenged powerfully. We are called ignorant if we believe in the Bible. Many scholars scoff at the thought of finding in an Intelligent Designer. The bad news is, it isn't going to get easier from here on out. I believe Christians are going to be challenged more and more in the future

In the last chapter of the Bible, Revelation 22, the phrase *"Behold I am coming soon"* appears three times. We cannot sit back and be indecisive regarding our beliefs nor on taking action for His kingdom. Have faith that He is indeed right there with you through all of the challenges as you boldly step forward in your Christian walk.

There are hundreds of verses in the Bible that spill over with encouraging statements, reminding us that God will never, ever leaves us. If you doubt this, grab your Bible and do a quick study on the number of verses claiming this truth.

Now is the time to make a decision regarding your faith and to move forward with conviction. This choice is ultimately yours to make. How will you answer?

"So do not fear, for I am with you; do not be dismayed, for I am your God. I will strengthen you and help you; I will uphold you with my righteous right hand" (Isaiah 41:10).

THEOSYNTHESIS®

PART V
ULTIMATE CARE OF SELF

CHAPTER 24
CARING FOR YOUR TEMPLE & THEOSTASIS

WHEN YOU comprehend and believe your body is a temple, this knowledge changes the game. Looking great on the outside is not the only goal of health. Encompassing all areas of health and wellness should be a priority.

> *"Do you not know that your bodies are temples of the Holy Spirit, who is in you, whom you have received from God? You are not your own; you were bought at a price. Therefore honor God with your bodies" (1 Corinthians 6:19–20).*

Theosynthesis then is the care of the whole body, mind, and spirit. Each part is equally important and should be honored and cared for accordingly. No one part of this equation is more important than the others. Maintaining a balance was discussed in detail in Chapter 12. A balance or homeostasis in all areas of wellness is critically essential.

In writing this book, I began to see yet another word emerging, "theostasis." As the word "homeostasis" refers to balance within our bodies, theostasis would be the balance between the mind, body, and spirit. An imbalance in any one of these areas will result in disharmony.

All of these suggestions below need to be maintained in balance. Too much of a good thing can become an obsession which will lead to an imbalance in the other areas. Theostasis is the key to overall health and well-being. Let's break down each of these three aspects and explore them individually.

THE MIND

A mind out of sync or in poor health will not be able to maintain a complete Theosynthesis in the body. Keeping the brain healthy is something we need to be paying more attention to, especially as we age. There are many practical steps we can do to improve and maintain our minds.

The mind is not discussed much regarding specifics on how to maintain optimal health and wellness. Of course, what we read, see, and hear affects our thoughts; therefore, protecting what you are exposed to is essential.

Physiologically, the brain needs proper nutrition and rest. Feeding it begins with whole foods and an appropriate balance of vitamins and minerals. As you consciously consider what you are putting into your body, the question should be "Is this going to benefit or harm me?"

Limiting the toxins entering your body is also of great importance. The blood-brain barrier does a great job in the overall protection of the brain, yet many harmful chemicals cross directly into the brain and bathe it in toxic substances.

Overuse of alcohol and drugs are some of the most harmful substances to brain tissue. Toxic substances must be kept at a minimum if you are to maintain optimal brain and mental health. Without a healthy brain functioning at its full potential, an imbalance in your overall well-being will be created over time.

THE BODY

Most of us think of our outer physical body when we think about health and wellness. In this country, people are obsessed with how they look. As we have discussed in other chapters, this obsession with body image has created an entire generation of people so focused on the outside of their body that they have no time for the care of the mind or of their spiritual needs.

Scripture reminds us that our body is a temple, and this means it is to be used to honor God. Sadly, however, the aspect of educating people to honor their body is sorely missing in our churches today. If you took any segment of the population and assess its level of health and wellness, most likely, you would find there are more unhealthy and unfit people than healthy ones.

The American diet, lack of exercise, and sedentary jobs have created this chasm of overweight, unhealthy people. Even with all of the modern advances in medicine, our population is facing an all-time catastrophic health crisis. The statistics pointing to the increases in heart disease, cancer, diabetes, and high blood pressure are staggering.[1]

---

1   "How to Help Prevent Heart Disease at Any Age," https://www.heart.org/en/healthy-living/healthy-lifestyle/how-to-help-prevent-heart-disease-at-any-age, April 1, 2015.

It is also important to note that overuse or excessive exercise regime can also be detrimental. When exercise becomes the idol in life to the point of body worship, it will create problems in the long run. I've known many friends who have taken their love of exercise to a level of complete obsession. Their families, friends, and also work lives have suffered at some point. Although they were physically fit, other parts of the body are affected because they were neglected.

Please don't misunderstand me on this; training for a race or hitting a fitness goal is excellent. I am talking about when the exercise becomes the main obsession in life. It's all they talk about and think about all day. Often when a person gets to this point of extreme focus on a sport or activity, it might be time to look inward to discover if they might be running from something else.

In the same manner, everything you eat and drink will affect every part of your body. As fast-food emerged in our country, we now see the effects on our people as morbid obesity is rampant. Even very young children are suffering from obesity in shocking numbers.

I'll be discussing food in Chapter 27 in much greater detail. In this chapter, we will be focusing on the importance of maintaining a balance of what you use to fuel your body. The primary purpose of food is for fuel and nutrition. Sadly, though, food has become a luxury that is over-indulged and misused.

With an automobile, if you choose to put inferior gasoline products into your car, you will begin to see problems. Before too long, engine parts will break down, and the vehicle will not run how it was designed. Why on Earth then, do we not take more care with the most important of engines—our own bodies?

It always surprises me when people are shocked to get diagnosed with a disease such as type 2 diabetes. When they are overweight, make poor dietary choices, and spend very little time, if any at all, exercising, why should diabetes be a surprise?

This amazing body we have been given is capable of a lifetime of use if we feed and care for it properly. A constant diet of sodas (and yes, even the diet ones), highly processed foods with no real nutritional value, and a steady stream of preservatives in our food bathe every cell of the body with harmful substances.

The body does the best it can to regulate itself and is continually trying to maintain homeostasis, but like the engine in the car, without proper care and nutrients, those beautifully designed parts begin to malfunction. Diseases of the organs start making us sick.

Unfortunately, many people head to their doctor to be placed on medication. When no lifestyle changes occur, they become slaves to a particular drug and all of its side effects for the rest of their lives. If you are sick, understanding why and then taking measures to correct the problem is where medical care should be directing and educating people.

Overall health and well-being of the body is a choice. Your bones and joints are designed to function correctly at an optimal weight. Always remaining in an overweight state puts tremendous stress and pressure on these mechanical body parts. Eventually, as the body becomes heavier and heavier, the strain on these bones will be more than they can withstand.

We all know when our body is not well; it is tough to pay attention to the mind and the spirit. When you hurt or are uncomfortable, it can keep your focus only on your pain and discomfort. An unhealthy state isn't fun and will keep you in an overall imbalance.

I recently was inspired by a story I read about an 86-year-old woman named Jessica Slaughter, who was obese most of her life.

When she reached the age of 70, her doctor told her she was prediabetic. She vowed right then to make some changes.

She first changed her diet to mostly vegan, and then she started wanting to exercise. She didn't want to go to a gym, and going outside by herself was not an option either. Therefore, she just started walking in her one-bedroom home. Just getting up and moving her body was the goal.

> "I walk 3,000 steps every morning before I start walking elsewhere," Slaughter said. "You don't have to go fast to get into shape; you just have to go. I want seniors to know that just because we've reached a certain age, we don't have to stop living. There's a better way of life if they choose it."[2]

Jessica Slaughter should be an inspiration to all of us. She was determined to make the changes necessary for her health, and then she followed through with an action plan. Additionally, she stuck with it. Over time, she watched her body shed the unnecessary pounds, and through the healthy food choices, changed her health from the inside out.

She looks fantastic, but more importantly, she is living! She said, "We don't have to stop living!" She gets it. Just existing with a body that can no longer function properly is not living. Now, however, she has chosen to live and to be fully alive.

THE SPIRIT

---

2   Zee Krstic, "An 86-Year-Old Woman Lost 120 Pounds by Doing This Simple Thing Every Day," https://www.cookinglight.com/news/how-to-lose-weight-walking, January 17, 2019.

This area of spiritual health is probably one of the most overlooked areas. Our spiritual side is such a private part of us and is the least understood. The main principle of this entire book is maintaining a connection to God. Today, we are losing a substantial spiritual battle for our souls.

As I researched this particular chapter, I googled the phrase "spiritual health." The first page of articles focused on the spirit as possessing a sense of well-being or happiness, almost like a how-to regarding emotional health. Being happy is great, yet, I am referring to connecting your spiritual self to God.

People are misled by a trend in honoring "spirit," which has nothing at all to do with God or Jesus. The spirit they are referring to is sometimes meaning their own spiritual god within themselves. They worship secular humanism rather than the God of the universe.

As a Christian, the more sanctified we become in our life with Him, the more radiant and brighter the emotional and spiritual parts of you become. Taking the time to place our focus on God rather than on ourselves will help us face the severe issues of this life with clear thinking. As we put our faith in God, our spirits will be lifted rather than being mired down with the negative aspects of life.

Also, as we gain the mind of Christ, we learn to lean on Him and not on our understanding. The Holy Spirit fills us and becomes our guide as we navigate our lives.

> *"Trust in the Lord with all your heart and lean not on your own understanding; in all your ways submit to Him, and He will make your paths straight"* (Proverbs 3:5–6).

I often hear the saying, "So and so is such a good Christian."

Saying this implies there is such a thing as a "bad Christian." Sure, Christians can and will do bad things, but saying they are a terrible Christian means that we can turn from being Christians into something that goes against God.

The reason I bring this up is to make the point that when we have earnestly accepted Christ into our lives, and we are filled with His Spirit, we possess His fantastic gift. It cannot be taken from us.

A spirit after God's heart will bear what is referred to as the fruit of the Spirit. "*But the fruit of the Spirit is love, joy, peace, forbearance, kindness, goodness, faithfulness, gentleness, and self-control*" (Galatians 5:22–23). If we could master all of these attributes, wouldn't our lives be so much more peaceful and fulfilled?

I love how these attributes are compared to fruit. Fruit means life, production, and harvest. These attributes provide us with the tools we need in this life. The opposite of life is death, a nonproducing life without a harvest. Therefore, these attributes cause death to the spirit.

Meditate on the fruitfulness of the spirit's attributes and put them into action. Replacing words of life will fill your spirit with the heart of God. In this manner, you can grow in your spirit and experience a God-balance or theostasis.

Here are some practical steps to maintain this state of balance:

MEDITATION AND PRAYER. Being quiet and still before the Lord is a must. The research shows the physical benefits of quieting the mind, body, and spirit each day. (See chapter 13 for more on this topic.)

REGULAR EXERCISE. Don't let me lose you with this topic. You do not need to become a marathon runner!

The studies are compelling on the overall benefits to the mind by just taking a pleasant brisk walk each day.

REST. If we don't allow our mind, body, and spirit time to rest, we will burn out and be useless to God, our families, and ourselves. A refreshed soul can accomplish what you were created to do. In the following chapter, we will discuss rest at length.

PROPER NUTRITION. The types of food you choose will determine your overall health. The saying, "You are what you eat" is correct. Chapter 27 is full of information regarding dietary choices.

FULFILLMENT. Doing whatever makes you happy is not the point. To be fulfilled means to accomplish and to achieve. Not all accomplishments are the big things in life. An accomplished and fulfilled life can mean having a satisfaction you are doing the work that has meaning for others and God. Discover what you like, and pursue it with all of your heart.

Your temple is a precious gift from God. Honoring this body He gave you will help you lead the life you desire and to fulfill what He ordained for you. A healthy temple is one that can serve God and others for a lifetime. May you decide today as Jessica Slaughter did that this is your day to make a change.

CHAPTER 25

REST

A H H H , THE CHAPTER on rest! I love to rest and begin a new day feeling refreshed. Necessary rest has been the one area many people sacrifice to work longer hours or to fit in more things to do during the day. In this chapter, we will discuss the various types of rest.

First, let's define "rest."

The Merriam-Webster Dictionary has many definitions for rest:

- a bodily state with minimal function and slower metabolic activities
- freedom from activity or labor
- state of motionless or inactivity
- peace of mind or spirit

Now, let's take a look at specific types of rest:

SLEEP

The human body needs an average of six to eight hours of sleep each day for optimal health. Throughout your life, these sleep variables can change. Babies sleep a lot as they are experiencing tremendous growth. When you are sick or recovering from an injury or surgery, you will also require more sleep for the body to repair itself.

Sleep provides our bodies with natural repair, rest for joints, muscles, and bones, and regulation of the chemicals in the body. A good night's rest is essential for overall health and wellness. A continuous lack of sleep will be a detriment to your health over time.

Sleep deprivation affects every part of your body. If you are not able to maintain basic sleep patterns, you eventually will pay the price with your health. If you have difficulties sleeping, discovering the reason for the lack of sleep is essential.

Being overweight will also affect sleep patterns negatively. Additional pounds create more weight on the organs, such as the heart and lungs, even while lying down. Additionally, the extra weight means your body is carrying more toxins that the body tries to rid itself of during sleep. More toxins mean more work for your sleeping body.

Nutrition, of course, affects your sleep. Too much caffeine, sugar, artificial flavorings, and other chemicals will disrupt sleep patterns. Eliminating as many of these toxins from your diet will have very positive effects on your ability to be able to sleep well.

Carrying much emotional stress will also affect quality sleep. As we have discussed throughout this book, continuous pressure will negatively affect your overall health. Taking your problems to bed with you and allowing your mind to focus on them will certainly keep you from the rest your body needs.

Learning some positive habits for handling the stress in your life is very important to sleeping well. Turning off the TV at bedtime, reading something inspirational, praying, and listening to calming music are all ways in which you can help your mind rest as you go to sleep. I enjoy falling asleep thinking about the things for which I am thankful.

> "A great windstorm arose, and the waves were breaking into the boat so that the boat was already filling. But He (Jesus) was in the stern, asleep on the cushion" (Mark 4:37–38).

RELAXATION

Relaxation is very different from sleep. When you can rid yourself or be free for just a while from the stress and tension of everyday life, then you can experience relaxation. Being able to sit quietly and learning how to unwind effectively is essential.

I'm not sure where and when we as Americans started viewing relaxation as a bad thing. When we feel guilty for taking out time for a break, guilt is created. And guess what? It is all right to relax, and it is a much-needed activity in this crazy, stress-filled world we live.

Permit yourself to take daily breaks. Go for a walk. Do a crossword puzzle, read a book, or be still and do nothing at all.

True relaxation is not laziness unless it becomes your norm. Your mental and physical health will improve as you learn to let go and allow some time for stillness. Why not give it a try?

> "Very early in the morning, while it was still dark, he departed and went out to a desolate place, and there he prayed" (Mark 1:35).

ACTIVE REST

Active resting is what we call having fun. What causes you to smile and laugh? When do we as adults stop playing? As children, we instinctively know how to play because it is a natural activity. Children naturally skip about, laughing, and playing.

Each of us should slow down enough to learn how to play again. Games, skipping, swinging, hopping, jumping, exploring are all great ways to get back to the act of playing. If you have grandchildren or children, get out there and play with them!

Active rest is excellent for the soul. Allowing yourself to play without guilt is the rule. How are you going to play today?

"Then it happened that as Jesus was reclining at the table in the house, behold, many tax collectors and sinners came and were dining with Jesus and His disciples" (Matthew 9:10).

SOCIAL REST

Being around other people can energize us and give us a break from our routines. Human connections are sometimes the very best thing we need. Of course, as in anything, too much can be exhausting.

Determine the people who bring you joy, build you up, and make you smile. Plan times to be together socially. Have small groups of friends over to your home where more intimate conversations can happen.

A stable social life does not depend on spending a ton of money. Look for ways to spend time with your friends that don't cost anything more than the time you will be spending. Parks, walking, book clubs, and card games are all ways to spend quality social time without breaking the bank.

SABBATICAL

I have always wanted to truly get away and do nothing else but read, write, and think. However, this escape has always felt like a luxury, leaving me feeling guilty for desiring a mental break. For many, a big project, a creative process, or the need to heal are great reasons to extend your time away, which is different from a vacation.

I'll never forget when my husband encouraged me to take the time away to complete this book. One night he said, "I know you want to finish your book, and you can't get it done here. Why don't you go somewhere you can get it done?"

It was as if I had just received the best gift. I needed this encouragement to get away to achieve my goal. What a wonderful gift of a sabbatical that was immensely rewarding.

If you ever have the opportunity to take a sabbatical, do it! Plan when you will go, make the necessary budget to make it happen, and then dive in and go without any guilt. I promise it will be the best thing you could ever give to yourself!

"One of those days, Jesus went out to a mountainside to pray, and spent the night praying to God" (Luke 6:12).

God created us to rest. Even He rested after He created the world. The Bible is full of Scripture related to rest. He is our guide on this, and there is a reason He created rest. Make sure you are balancing your life with the rest needed!

CHAPTER 26

GREEN ESSENTIALS

YOU MIGHT BE wondering why I have a chapter entitled "Green Essentials" and why I have also included the following section on nutrition and fuel. While these topics may seem similar, I believe you will understand why I felt the need to keep them in separate chapters.

In this chapter, I am specifically referring to the fantastic benefits we derive from plants God placed on this earth as a food source as well as other significant benefits to us. A closer look at these beautiful green plants is needed to gain a full appreciation of them and how they impact our lives.

There is no accident in Genesis 1:11–12 that tells us, *"Then God said, 'Let the land produce vegetation; seed-bearing plants and trees that bear fruit with seed in it.' And it was so. The land produced vegetation: plants bearing seed according to their kind."* Then fast forward to verses 29 and 30: *"Then God said, 'I give you every seed-bearing plant on the face of the whole earth, and every tree that has fruit with seed in it. They will be yours for food....I give every green plant for food....."*

Following in Genesis 2:8–9, *"No, the Lord God had planted a garden in the east, in Eden; there He put the man He had formed. And the Lord God made all kinds of trees grow out of the ground—trees that were pleasing to the eye and good for food.....*"

God's order for His creation was to place the plants on Earth even before Adam came to being. God made sure everything we needed for healthy living was already set in place before He also created man. He said in 1:30, "*...I give every green plant for food.....*" Therefore, all we need on this earth is already here.

A quick review of botany allows us to have a close and personal glimpse into the world of plants. As we know, life on this earth would not be possible without plants. As humans, we depend on the plants, and they, in turn, rely on us, thereby, creating a symbiotic relationship where both derive a benefit from the other.

The fantastic exchange of oxygen is a gift from the plants to humans and other animals, while carbon dioxide is a gift from us to the plants. This cycle is pure genius. This necessary process is called "photosynthesis." However, most of us miss what a genuinely intricate and beautiful process it is that could have only come about by a magnificent designer.

The most basic structures of a plant include the main anatomical structures of the seed, which springs forth life, roots, stems, leaves, flowers, and fruits. Each of these structures in and of themselves is remarkably intricate and complex and vitally important for the plant to grow and thrive properly.

Plants provide a variety of essential processes to the earth, animals and man:

- Exchange of life-giving gases of oxygen and carbon dioxide
- Food
- Regulation of the water cycle via transpiration, the process

of a plant moving water from the soil to the atmosphere and helping to purify water

- Medicine
- Drought and erosion of soil assistance
- Material for clothing, timber, paper
- Animal habitats
- Fuels

For me, the most fantastic process plants go through is photosynthesis. The fact that a plant can convert sunlight into food is miraculous. This process alone points to an apparent intelligent designer. In college, I thought I would quickly zip through botany class. It wasn't long before I began seeing a much bigger picture, and I gained more understanding and appreciation of photosynthesis.

In a nutshell, the energy from the sun is collected via amazing little structures in the leaf of plants called "chloroplasts." As the light energy is accumulated inside of these structures, the light is then converted through a fantastic chemical process into chemical compounds called "carbohydrates." These carbohydrates or sugars are substances that provide humans and animals with food.

Doesn't that blow your mind? The sun's rays shining down on us are converted into food. We, therefore, nourish our bodies with the fuel of the sun. Amazing!

Additionally, the extraction of chemical substances from plants and the use of various plant parts also provide us with healing medicines, poultices, and vapors. Prior to modern medicine, herbalists or plant specialists studied the different plants to determine how to use them effectively for illnesses, injuries, and overall well-being.

Over the years, modern medicine evolved and began moving

into the pharmaceutical industry where plants are utilized to create chemical compounds we call "medicine." The origin of the word "pharmacy" is interesting. The Greek root *pharmakeia* meant the use of drugs, medicines, potions, or spells—poisoning, witchcraft, remedy, or cure.[1] A pharmakeus was a preparer of medications, poisoners, sorcerer, or preparer of spells.

Obviously over time, this word has evolved into the pharmaceutical meaning it has today, which refers to the preparation and prescribing of medicines for use in illness and disease. I do find it interesting that the origin of this word referred to potions and witchcraft. More on the topic this later in the book.

Initially, the practice of medicine was deeply tied to spiritual beliefs. In ancient Israel, the priests were the doctors while amongst native American tribes, the physicians were called the medicine man or woman. Healing was done with God as an involved partner.

As medicine modernized, it has moved completely out of the realm, which includes any mention of God at all. As God has slowly been removed from our schools and our universities, there are no longer any teachings that include both God and medicine. As man continues to remove God from education and politics, the ability to weave biblical beliefs with medicine is not likely.

Indeed, we have seen a lot of wonderful discoveries in the evolvement of medicine. Great strides through modern medicine have helped numerous people overcome sicknesses, injuries, and other maladies. What I am referring to here are the many physicians and pharmacists who do not connect medicine to God. These professionals do not see the importance of this connection. Those who see and understand the God-connection are treated with indifference or

---

1   https://biblehub.com/greek/5331.htm.

ignored, and many times, shunned.

God placed everything we need on this earth to survive and thrive; therefore, it makes sense to include Him as we seek to understand His fantastic creation further. Recently, many professionals in the medical field began to open their minds to alternative and holistic treatments. Hopefully, more will embrace some of the more natural approaches and integrate these practices into modern medicine.

Fortunately, many medical professionals do agree in combining natural healing methods with modern medicine. It is essential to also understand that a single type of healing method is not always the answer. Therefore, keeping an open mind to experiment with alternative methods should be embraced.

Another area where the medical industry has taken a turn is the fact that it has become a dominant force politically and economically. Medicine and pharmaceutical drugs are huge businesses, and many in this industry desire is to see a profit, regardless of those people who are hurt in their wake.

The problem is when the profit of a drug becomes more important than the potential lives it could potentially harm. The drug industry must take responsibility for the substances they are creating and take great care to ensure these drugs are more helpful than they are harmful.

A pharmaceutical drug is a chemical compound made in a laboratory. Because these chemical compounds are not natural to the human body, there will always be side effects when they are taken. It is essential to know

The problem is when the profit of a drug becomes more important than the potential lives it could potentially harm.

the pros and cons of any drug we choose to ingest into our bodies.

Please understand, I'm not trying to bash this industry entirely. Many significant advances in modern medicine have saved many lives. I'm trying to bring about an awareness of the limits of modern drugs and the precautions we should know about them. Specifically, many people begin taking medications for long-term use rather than finding ways to correct the problem, which created the issue of needing the drug.

A pharmaceutical drug can help a person overcome an illness. However, continuous drug use can lead to long-term effects and secondary health issues that can create problems. Rather than seeking ways to correct diseases that came about because of our neglect, many rely on the extended use of medications.

As I wrote earlier, people are now taking drugs with harmful side effects for a lifetime. In doing this, they are not taking responsibility for lifestyle changes, nor is the medical community encouraging patients to make changes to eventually get off the drugs. This approach is not health care; instead, this is "sick care."

Additionally, I find it upsetting how the Food and Drug Administration is not a friend to those who choose to practice natural medicine or who are utilizing natural herbs and plants to assist in medical ailments. Websites, social media pages, and advocates for alternative health methods are being shut down at alarming rates! This fact alone should be shocking and concerning to all of us in this country.

Those who choose a natural regimen route for illnesses and disorders are considered to be engaging in quackery. Because the more natural approach does not require spending an arm and a leg on drugs, the big companies do not benefit. Therefore, they see these other methods as a threat to their bottom line.

Seriously, at what cost? Sadly, at the expense of many, many lives of people who die every day from the harmful side effect of a man-made pharmaceutical drug. Yes, there have been people who have perished from misusing natural remedies; however, the statistics from recent pharmaceutical deaths are far higher than the more natural approaches.

We need to allow each person to choose their method of healing. Should they accept the modern medicine route, this should be respected and honored. Likewise, adopting a more natural, holistic approach should also be a choice that is equally respected and honored.

Most natural choices, however, are not covered by insurance and are frowned upon by those in modern medicine. As a result, this forces most people to seek the modern medicine approach and the pharmaceutical-driven machine. The natural healing choices must be paid directly out of pocket, which is difficult for most people.

Taking a hard look at the power that plants possess and what they can do for us should be an option that comes without a penalty for those who choose this route. I have had to increase my learning about more natural options out there as modern drugs cause severe reactions within me. I have turned to more natural choices, yet I haven't experienced any of those same reactions I did when using new chemical compounds.

Not only do I feel better without taking daily drugs, but my health and well-being also have never been better, even at the age of 59. It has taken me years of study to seek out answers for my health needs. The more I continue to learn, the more convinced I am of being on the right track.

In writing this chapter, I know there will be many people who will choose to criticize me for speaking my truth. Many natural health professionals have been bullied and shut down by those desiring to control all of the health-care industry. My main message to each one of you reading this is to seek your answers and base your decisions on what you feel is the best option for you.

Don't forget, however, that as a believer, God gave us minds to use, ask questions, and seek the truth. He has given us beautiful, healing plants for our benefit. It is our responsibility to gain an understanding of these plants and to learn what they can do for us.

Do your own research. Read whatever you can, and then step boldly and confidently in the choices you make. Remember, your body is a temple and was created to be used in God's kingdom. Perhaps what you need for optimal health is growing in the soil right now.

CHAPTER 27

NUTRITION & FUEL

HAVING A GOOD understanding of the food supply God prepared and placed on Earth will allow us to focus on adequately utilizing this food so it can provide us with the proper nutrition as it was created to do. My hope and prayer are to open your eyes to see food in a new way.

In my lifetime (now, six decades), I have watched the type of food we ingest in this county change dramatically. As a little girl growing up in the '60s and '70s, fast food was coming on the market as a new and convenient way to eat. For most families, eating out or being able to dine on fast foods was not a regular event.

First of all, it was more expensive to eat out than it was to cook and prepare your own food. Therefore, we ate home-cooked meals much more than we ever went out to eat. During my college years, it was a luxury to eat at a restaurant. Thankfully, I didn't have the opportunity to eat a lot of highly processed foods.

Today for most families, the way we eat has changed completely. Rather than home-cooked meals, eating out is the norm. Fast food has become the standard as families race about with their busy schedules. We as a society are seeing the detrimental long-term health effects of these dietary choices.

The obesity rate continues to soar in this country as we move further away from the food God created for us to eat to foods that have very little if any nutritional value.[1] We are filling our bodies with extremely high amounts of preservatives, additives, fillers, sugars, and chemicals. Because we were not designed to ingest these ingredients, our health and well-being are suffering.

What saddens me the most is the number of young children who are already morbidly obese at an early age. The increase in the obesity rate in children today is painfully obvious. And this is *not okay!* It is not healthy for any of us to be morbidly obese.

I say all of this with genuine compassion and sensitivity. I am not desiring to bash those who are battling the disease of obesity. I *am*, however, placing the blame where it should be—the food industry. There is currently an epidemic in our county, and that is an obesity issue.

We are duped into thinking processed foods are safe to consume. Sure, these highly processed foods are convenient; however, they are absolutely the worst things we can be putting into our bodies. At what cost then are we willing to compromise our health and well-being just for the sake of convenience?

Today for most families, the way we eat has changed completely. Rather than home-cooked meals, eating out is the norm. Fast food has become the standard as families race about with their busy schedules. We as a society are seeing the detrimental long-term health effects of these dietary choices.

---

1   Craig M. Hales, M.D., Margaret D. Carroll, M.S.P.H., Cheryl D. Fryar, M.S.P.H., and Cynthia L. Ogden, Ph.D., "Prevalence of Obesity and Severe Obesity Among Adults: United States," 2017–2018, NCHS Data Brief No. 360, https://www.cdc.gov/nchs/products/databriefs/db360.htm, February 2020.

Hopefully, this chapter is a wake-up call to us all. Each of us has choices regarding what we eat every day. Our children, however, do not have these free choices. They are guided and influenced by their parents, thereby becoming a product of these dietary choices. They depend on parents to guide them, and this includes nutritional decisions.

As a nation, we must recognize that there is a problem in the way we consume food. We must insist on educational awareness for the proper nutrition that both parents and children need for optimal health. Additionally, the food industry itself should also be held accountable for the types and quality of food they produce.

Like anything else, moderation is the key with our food choices. Just as an extreme diet can be detrimental, finding the right balance for nutritional needs is essential. A good rule of thumb is to eat as clean as you can. Clean eating includes fresh fruits and vegetables along with antibiotic-free meats. If you are craving sugars or carbs, satisfy these craving with a taste or two of the desired food but leave it at that.

During my presentations regarding wellness and nutrition, I often hear, "Organic foods are just too expensive"; "I can't afford to eat in this manner." Many people become hung up on how expensive it is to buy organic foods. With a little planning, discovering local farmer's markets and other creative purchasing options, learning to eat clean is doable.

My response is this: "Let me tell you what expensive resembles! Losing a lung is expensive. Being sick is costly." Take a look in your medicine cabinet and add up the costs of what you take daily as a result of a neglected body. Research the cost of surgery and illness due to obesity and nutrition deprivation. You will discover that being sick is way more expensive than staying healthy.

I recently saw a post on social media where someone put a picture of a popular fast-food hamburger. They unwrapped the burger, and it appeared someone had already taken a bite of it. The caption said, "Hey when I unwrapped this, it looks partially eaten. Should I eat it or throw it out?"

My first reaction was, of course, throw it out regardless if someone else has already taken a bite out of it. The point is, this is dead, toxic food, and you don't need it! There is nothing alive in these types of food at all. It is offering your body a lot of empty calories while providing you zero nutritional value.

Let's talk for a moment about foods in these terms of being alive or dead. Live foods are fresh fruits, vegetables, nuts, and seeds. They're eaten in their naturally harvested state and offer our body the vitamins, minerals, and trace elements needed for optimum nutrition. They are alive!

Fresh foods in their natural state also provide the roughage our digestive systems must have to function correctly. Our digestive tract is not designed for foods that remain in our gut for days on end. When food remains in the intestinal tract for long periods, fermentation, bacterial growth, and vast amounts of toxic gases are produced.

Processed foods full of preservatives, fillers, and chemicals do not pass through the human intestinal tract properly. These types of foods create a food mass that is extremely difficult to move through the system efficiently. The mixture becomes something like a toxic soup sludge that moves very slowly through the intestines and becomes a breeding ground for many illnesses.[2]

---

2   F. Kong and R.P. Singh. http://ucce.ucdavis.edu/files/datastore/608-87.pdf, Disintegration of Solid Foods in Human Stomach Journal of Food Science—Vol. 73, Nr. 5, 2008.

The intestinal wall is lined richly with blood vessels allowing nutrients from food to be broken down to a chemical level. Then these food molecules can be transported to every cell within our body. If you are pouring toxic chemicals such as junk or dead food into your body, your system is creating a sludge mixture coating the entire length of your intestinal tract. Yuck!

Once this happens, your intestinal tract is then no longer able to function in its intended purpose which is to break down foods, deliver nutrients, and expel wastes. Instead, the system works overtime trying to process this dead food, which contains zero nutrients and thereby creates a ton of waste. All of this gunk sits in the gut, causing a clogged and bloated system.

Think about this; if your car is continually filled with inferior gas and oil products, sludge builds up over time, causing the vehicle to no longer function properly. Isn't your body a much more valuable machine than your car? Each of us must take a hard look at the nutritional choices we are making. We need to come to a place where we honor ourselves enough to stop this madness.

If you are a parent of young children, you are ultimately responsible for how your child is being fed. If you make poor nutritional choices for them, you are choosing to expose your children to the same diseases that will ultimately destroy their health and well-being. Parents, this is on you!

Yes, I am writing this with a strong voice because I am angry with what I am witnessing in our so-called "affluent" society. People are being duped into thinking it is all right to be overweight and eat processed products mislabeled as food. The highly processed foods on the shelves today are closer to being in the same chemical makeup as plastics.

So, yes, I will take much heat for speaking my mind in this chapter. However, for those of you reading this, if you are honest, you know this information is accurate. If you have become complacent in watching people around you throwing away their health and perhaps your health, you are choosing to stick your head in the sand. If you are sick, tired, and overweight due to poor nutritional choices, you can choose today to stop this madness.

Your body was not designed to handle foods loaded with preservatives. Amazingly, your body is brilliantly able to fight off and correct itself for a while. However, as you continue to pollute the system, it will be a matter of time before your body, this amazing gift from God, becomes so polluted and sick, it can no longer keep up.

In addition to creating a sluggish intestinal tract, in the absence of necessary nutrients, every physiological process in your body will receive very little useful fuel. Without fuel or energy, it becomes difficult to achieve maximum mental and physical capacity. Also, the ability of the body to receive nutrients to maintain and repair your body correctly is altered. Basically, without proper nutrition, your body becomes rundown, haggard, and sick.

If we are created in God's image and are here to make a difference in His kingdom, doesn't it make sense to do whatever you can to maintain your optimal health? If you are sluggish, tired, in pain, and sick, it will be much more challenging to do what God created you to do. You may be

If we are created in God's image and are here to make a difference in His kingdom, doesn't it make sense to do whatever you can to maintain your own optimal health?

prevented from doing some amazing things for His kingdom because you continue to make poor nutritional choices in your life.

Hear me on this: I am not throwing every unhealthy person under the bus. We all have the propensity to become ill. Bacterial and viral illnesses will affect our lives. However, a body that has been adequately fed will be able to fight off and recover from this illness much faster than a body receiving very little whole and living food.

When I refer to sick people in this chapter, I am specifically referring to those people experiencing illnesses due to neglect and poor nutritional choices. Many individuals are doing amazing things for this world, even though they are ill or perhaps in a wheelchair. I am not talking about these types of maladies. My point here is taking personal responsibility regarding the nutritional choices we have every day.

If you are suffering right now due to the effects of poor nutritional choices, today is the day to make a change. Right now, decide you have had enough! This very moment, it can start with you and with your choices.

Remember, as a Christian, you do have an obligation to take care of the gift that has blessed you properly. YOU are the gift specially created by God! If you genuinely believe we are made in His image, You are His. This thought alone should be extremely convicting.

Let me ask you a question. Have you ever received a beautiful gift you truly cherished? I would venture to guess you took great care of this object. You most likely placed it in a safe place so it wouldn't get broken. This precious and valued object was most likely treated with the utmost care and concern.

Isn't your own body way more valuable than any object or thing on this earth? Shouldn't you take great care of this fantastic structure you've been placed in your care? The greatest of value should be placed on yourself as you recognize and accept this truth.

I hope this chapter kicked you in the butt. Yes, there it is. I said it. Sometimes we all need a big can of "whoop ass!"

It's time to stop making excuses and begin taking charge of your beautifully designed, fantastic self. You are worth it. It is never too late to decide to honor your precious health.

CHAPTER 28

EXERCISE & MOVEMENT

WHEW! I know that the last chapter was difficult for many to read and digest. (Pun fully intended!) As I wrote it, I felt utterly convicted to lay it on. As a society, we have turned the other cheek for too long.

Now on to another critical topic—exercise and movement. I can hear you inwardly groaning and saying, "No, I don't wanna sweat, and I don't want to do the work it'll take to get my body in shape."

Stay with me, folks. Maintaining a properly fed and fueled-up body is necessary, but it is also critical to keep this machine oiled and in peak condition. A well-fed body must also move to be appropriately "oiled."

The human body was not designed to be sedentary. This amazingly complex structure we live in was designed with strong muscles, bones, and ligaments allowing us to move in all sorts of surprising ways. Not all of us will have incredible strength, flexibility, or stamina, but we have been gifted with a physical structure that allows us to do amazing things.

Your body is a gift, and if you allow it to remain stagnant and unused, it will not be able to serve you properly for a lifetime. The same car analogy we referred to previously applies to this topic as well. If our bodies are ignored, not given the care and maintenance required, it will eventually rust and break down. Just like the car will need to be driven, tuned up, lubricated, and maintained to regularly get from point A to B, your body requires this same care.

Your body is a gift, and if you allow it to remain stagnant and unused, it will not be able to serve your properly for a lifetime.

If you have chosen a life of physical inactivity, you will eventually be faced with a body that is not capable of carrying you from point A to B. Those inactive muscles will become weak and prone to injury if they are not utilized properly. Joints and tendons stiffen up, thereby not able to serve you well if they remain inactive.

Even people who suffer from arthritic and muscular diseases can benefit from some movement. Those who cannot exercise the way they used to can and will benefit from exercises done in water or non-weight-bearing activities. Physical therapists work with patients after surgery to increase the range of movement for the recovering ailment. These professionals know that mobility is essential to the future healing and use of the affected area.

In college, I was impressed with a young man I knew named Chris. He was a vibrant individual who would talk your ear off, was the life of the party, and made the best of any situation. You see, Chris was injured in his teenage years in a horrific car accident that left him paralyzed from the waist down. Chris was now in a wheelchair.

His wheelchair, however, did not define him. I remember vividly going to the student recreation center with him to watch him swim laps. He would get his wheelchair as close to the pool as possible and then slide down into the water and swim lap after lap using only his arms.

Chris taught me a valuable lesson. Although his legs were now useless, he was determined to keep his body in the best possible condition he could. It would have been easy for him to make excuses, but he didn't choose to live this way.

I believe that his determination to stay in top condition positively affected his mental and emotional states. Rather than sit there and lament on the what-ifs, he made the choice he would not be a victim. He chose to move!

When I lost a huge chunk of my left lung at the age of 50 due to the massive tumor, it would have been easy to say, "I'll never run again." I won't lie and say the recovery process was easy because it was hell getting myself back into shape. It was a painful process.

Thankfully, I decided to get up and move one step at a time. Chris was always on my mind during those tough days. When I didn't want to get up, I imagined Chris and his determination. He inspired me, and I will be eternally grateful for his encouragement to overcome.

On the other hand, exercise can become an obsession for some people. I am not suggesting nor encouraging people to exercise to the point of obsession. As mentioned earlier in this book, even too much of a good thing can be detrimental. As Theosynthesis, remember, is all about connecting and finding a balance.

The first step in changing your body through movement and exercise is simply deciding to do it. Without making a personal decision, no one can guilt you into jumping on the fitness wagon. This action is your decision alone and one I hope you will consider before your neglected body is unable to move at all.

The steps I am sharing with you are the ones I incorporated into my life as I recovered from lung surgery. Having to start all over after the surgery caused me to have to completely start over and step by step, regain my strength.

Honestly, this was one of the most challenging things I have ever done. My 50-year-old body was saying no while my emotionally, weary self was trying to convince me I had great excuses to sit and take it easy. Thankfully, I got up and began moving.

Hopefully, these steps will encourage you as you embark on your new journey to achieving a fit and robust body. I created a call-to-action list, "10 Steps to Move Forward." I hope these tips help motivate you to begin moving and feel your very best.

Whatever physical challenges you are faced with, it is never too late to take the first step. You are worth it! Your family is worth it! God has plans for your life. Will you boldly make the decision today to honor your body as you step out in faith in complete dedication to health and wellness?

10 Steps to Move Forward

1. Make the decision right now to start moving.

2. Be realistic in what type of exercise you are capable of doing right now. What are your limitations? Consider where you live, the weather restrictions, etc.

3. Decide on the time that will work with your schedule and determine how much time you can devote to your new movement schedule. Remember, start slowly and set your goals accordingly. Start with at least having the determination to move at least 3 days per week.

4. Tell your family, friends and co-workers what your goals are so they can help encourage you. Include those people who are encouraging rather than anyone who will discourage you from reaching your goals. There is absolutely no room for the negative Nellies!

5. Keep a movement journal. Create a wall chart or any other visual allowing you to see your goals as you begin this journey.

6. Set your milestones and celebrate them as they are reached. My first milestone while in the hospital, was getting to the bathroom by myself. Next, to the door to the room, then the hallway, and finally making a lap around the entire 9th floor of the Methodist Hospital wing. The nurses became my cheerleaders.

7. Allow yourself to properly rest. It is OK to take breaks and to nurse sore joints and muscles during this process. Learn to appreciate and indulge in a good Epsom salt bath as often as you like!

8. Eat properly and drink plenty of pure water.

9. Change up your movement goals. Walking is great, but as in any repetitive activity, it can get boring. Walk one day, do chair exercises another, or try stretching or swimming.

10. Don't give up! Setbacks are a part of the process. Just don't allow a setback to derail you entirely. As I encouraged my beat-up body to move and to learn how to breathe with much less lung function, there were days I just couldn't do it. I didn't give up though, and this alone was the most important step I took.

CHAPTER 29

CHEMICALS & TOXINS

I RECENTLY read a startling comment concerning the number of chemicals and toxins we are exposed to daily. They far exceed what our grandparents were exposed to in an entire lifetime.[1] Toxic chemicals are everywhere and are found in everything, including the skincare products you use, household cleaners, the air we breathe, water, and soil.

The list of so-called "acceptable" chemicals the U.S. allows into your products should concern each of us. It helps for you to know about these toxins and to educate yourself to understand what they are, how they negatively impact your life, and how to avoid them.

My quest to seek more information about the pollutants I was ingesting and putting on my body daily was the original inspiration for writing this book. As I was sharing the knowledge of what I had been doing to clean up the toxins I was being exposed to, it became a mission for me to tell others.

---

1   "A Benchmark Investigation of Industrial Chemicals, Pollutants, and Pesticides in Umbilical Cord Blood," Environmental Working Group, https://www.ewg.org/research/body-burden-pollution-newborns, July 14, 2005.

After experiencing two of the most bizarre and rare tumors that almost ended my life, I set out to seek some answers. It was important to me to investigate more thoroughly as the growing tumors were a mystery to the doctors in Houston, Texas. As a person who spent a lifetime on a quest for physical health, these rare tumors were indeed strange.

During one of the meetings with a team of physicians at MD Anderson Cancer Center, one of the doctors asked me to go home and look at the products I used every day. He wanted me to watch for these particular ingredients: paraben, glycol ethers, and triclosan. There are a whole host of other chemicals I could list, but these were the main culprits he wanted me to be aware of.

Being the research geek that I am, when I got home, I took out every item I used daily and began writing down the top ingredients from each of them. From the makeup, face creams, shampoos, lotions, perfumes, toothpaste, and laundry detergent I used, the list of scary chemical names on this list was staggering. As I began to research these chemicals, I quite literally became sick to my stomach.

Products I was purchasing and assuming were safe to use were actually dumping huge amounts of the toxins directly into my system each and every day! This event was a game changer for me.

Products I was purchasing and assuming were safe to use were actually dumping vast amounts of the toxins directly into my system every day. This event was a game changer for me. I grabbed a huge trash bag and threw away every bit of those toxic products!

I knew I was throwing away a ton of money with this project, yet the tumors that almost killed me and cost a ton of cash were enough for me to say, "I'm done!" I began a new journey to seek out products that were free of these nasty chemicals and was not stopping until I found them.

Unfortunately, I have run into many roadblocks along the way. Many people like myself who have decided to lessen the daily toxic exposure are finding they are not allowed to share their findings. Posting something on social media or writing a blog where they merely told their own stories would mysteriously get shut down. Way too many natural health practitioners are also being bullied into keeping their mouths shut as they offer alternatives to the mainstream products being pushed by the big companies.

Are you kidding me? I thought we lived in a free country? Nope! Not when it comes to speaking your mind about big businesses who make a lot of money creating mass amounts of products loaded with poisons.

I will not be naming specific products as a little research on your own will be eye-opening and hopefully cause you to re-evaluate the items you are using on yourself, on your children, and in your home. Read the labels. Know your products.

Regarding indoor health, the chemicals you spray, burn, and clean with in your home all end up mostly as tiny particles in your respiratory tract. These minute particles are deposited into every cell of your body.

Speaking of cells, they are amazing, complex structures. The outside of the cell is composed of a specialized membrane allowing smaller molecular particles to enter while keeping other substances out. This cellular membrane is the gatekeeper for the cell.

Chemicals in the air quickly pass through the cellular matrix entering directly into the cell. Many of the chemicals found in our everyday products are hormone-disrupting as well as neurotoxic.[2] Ultimately, this means many of these substances will cause the balance of your endocrine system that regulates hormones to be disturbed. Specifically, the disruption of the all-important endocrine system wreaks havoc on overall health.

The endocrine system is responsible for temperature regulation, growth, hormones, metabolism, as well as reproduction. A disruption of the glands in the endocrine system will cause many issues over the long run. Diabetes, thyroid disease, and Grave's disease are just a few of the maladies caused by a compromised endocrine system.

As we live in this world and are continually exposed to not only the toxins in our food and personal products, we are also assaulted by pollution occurring in the environment.

Many of the plastics we use daily also contain harmful substances leaching toxins into our food and drinks as these chemicals break down. While we are exposed to these toxins day in and day out, these chemicals build up over time in our cells, tissues, and in our brain.

Fat cells, or adipose cells, serve as storage for our bodies but also create storage for the toxins. Therefore, an excess of adipose tissue (fat), will result in a much more considerable amount of stored chemicals in your cells if you are overweight. These poisons expose your entire system to a constant flow of toxins.

To place a visual on this scenario, I'll share a story from my anatomy lab days in college. Our lab groups were each assigned a

2   "Endocrine Disruptors," National Institute of Environmental Health Sciences, https://www.niehs.nih.gov/health/topics/agents/endocrine/index.cfm, May 22, 2020.

human cadaver. Our job was to discover the cause of death through dissection. My group was awarded the morbidly obese corpse.

One of the most vivid lessons we learned was observing the bright yellow fat that covered all of the internal organs. Our gloves were greasy as we carefully explored the abdominal cavity. Excessive amounts of fat were wrapped around every single organ.

Seeing this firsthand was something I will never, ever forget. In that moment, I vowed never to allow my body to experience this. If more people could see what excessive fat looks like within themselves, they would be powerfully impacted.

Your body is such a genuinely fantastic and efficient structure. Did you know that within a matter of just a few minutes, the products you put on your skin or the food and drinks you ingest send molecules to every cell in your body? The next time you drink a soda, think about the toxic soup bath you are pouring into your cells.

Speaking of sodas, these are absolutely some of the worst products you can choose to put into your body. It pains me to see people downing diet sodas too. The amount of chemicals and artificial sugars in these drinks is astounding. Again, zero nutritional value whatsoever.

Artificial sweeteners are also highly toxic. A few years ago, I toured a company in Texas that makes and creates polymers. Polymers are units of bonded-together molecules such as plastics and other synthetic products. The tour of this company began in the lobby and featured the items it produced in various glass cabinets.

In one particular cabinet was a piece of cultured marble, a snowboard, and surprisingly, a packet of artificial sweetener. My curiosity was piqued, and I asked the gentleman giving us the tour if it meant all of the products in that case were derived from the same polymer structure. His answer was yes. My next question was, "Do you ingest that product?" He replied quickly with an absolute no! Hmm, food for thought.

What I've learned through my education of the leading chemical toxins to avoid has led me on a path of choosing products I can trust. Digging deeper into the chemical names that are changed to sound like something else is a common practice. Therefore, continue reading and asking questions as you search for truth in this area.

In the supplement section in the back of this book, I have included several links to products I have researched and personally use. Please note that this is not a ploy to sell you anything. I am incredibly choosy and have done my homework over the years. I am consistently asked to share what I have learned; therefore, feel free to view this list and check out the products.

If you are doing everything you can to take care of yourself, understanding the toxins you are being exposed to is as important as your dietary choices and exercise regimen. Just because a product sits on the shelf at the grocery store does not mean it is safe to consume. Read, read, and read some more!

Also, if you are pregnant, planning on becoming pregnant, or nursing a child, you should be even more vigilant in researching what goes in and on your body. A developing child's system is far more sensitive when it comes to toxic chemicals. Also, what a baby or child breathes while in the home is a significant concern.

Get rid of the chemical cleaning sprays, toxic candles, and scented room items. The indoor pollution problem these products cause is very concerning. There are less expensive ways to clean your home and make it smell great without using products containing harsh chemicals.

Here are some tips for detoxifying your life as well as a clean-living challenge:

- Replace the harsh chemical sprays and cleaners with plain water, vinegar, and lemon juice substitutes. You can make do-it-yourself cleaners very quickly and inexpensively.

- Remove the candles and the plug-in scented items. Diffusing therapeutic-grade essential oils (see the Appendix on this) is a much better way to make your home or office smell great without the harmful side effects.

- Evaluate the personal products you use daily. Deodorant, hair care, makeup, skincare, and certain kinds of toothpaste all need to be researched for the main ingredients they contain. Do a chemical inventory of every product in your home.

- Purchase products from a reputable company that openly shares their ingredients. Also, skincare products that sit on a shelf for long periods are a reasonably good indicator that they are full of preservatives.

- Ditch the sodas and food products that are pure junk food in nature. What a waste of calories and money as these products dump toxic sludge into your system.

- Choose laundry detergents and softeners without harsh chemicals. Clothing is worn next to your skin; therefore, make sure your clothing is also free of toxins.

- Reduce the plastic items you use with your food. Don't drink water from a water bottle that has been left in a hot car. Heat breaks down the plastic, thereby releasing toxins directly into the water.

- Avoid using a microwave as much as you can. If you do microwave food, use ceramic dishes rather than plastics as the same principle applies to the heating of plastic containers.

- Beware of perfumes and colognes. Most of these products contain very high amounts of harmful toxins.

- Choose natural remedies to use in your gardens and yards. Bug and weed killers will eventually leach into the soil, thus affecting the groundwater. If you grow a personal edible garden, you must be super-vigilant in what you choose to put on your plants.

As in the previous chapters in this book on foods and exercise, you must use good, common sense of what works for you and your family. Each area is essential, and making changes to your entire home and lifestyle will take time. I do urge you to remove the most aggressive and caustic chemicals in your home immediately.

You can successfully take on a clean-living challenge if done one room at a time. Decide to take the first step— evaluating what chemicals are lurking in the products you are using daily. By identifying more natural products, you can then begin to replace the scary ones with safer choices.

Attend wellness workshops, join a social media group focused on clean living, and get your home and your life onto a road of healthier and safer choices. Your skin, your cells, and your overall health will be significantly impacted for the better when you make the needed changes.

Make sure and check out the Index in the back of this book for a list of some great companies that are committed to the products they produce. Best of luck to you as you begin taking steps to clean up your act.

CHAPTER 30

EMOTIONAL HEALTH

AS WE CONTINUE exploring the various areas of health and wellness in this book, we will now take a look at another critical area of overall health. We clearly illustrated in previous chapters that our bodies are a true gift from God. Every aspect of our fantastic structure has been perfectly designed. It is our responsibility to care for our overall health and well-being.

What then does well-being mean? It is possible to have a physically healthy body yet do very little to protect our minds from chemicals and drugs that damage brain cells. Additionally, Chapter 33 discusses the power of words. The effects of our private thoughts and words do affect mental health.

Theosynthesis, as we have discussed in various illustrations throughout this book, encompasses every aspect of our lives. It is completeness and a connection within our physical health, our spiritual health, and our emotional health. When one or more of these areas are not in optimum health, all of the other parts are affected.

"Do not be anxious about anything, but in everything by prayer and supplication with thanksgiving let your requests be made known to God. And the peace of God, which surpasses all understanding, will guard your hearts and your minds in Christ Jesus" (Philippians 4:6–7).

The keyword in this Philippians verse is the word "anxious." It is derived from the Latin word *anxius* from *angere* "to choke," strangle, or to be distressed. Choke and strangle are quite descriptive terms in this verse. When we remain in an anxious, stressed-out state, it is not suitable for our overall emotional well-being.

There is evidence of many people, both Christians and non-Christians, suffering from the effects of anxiety and stress. The statistics of the number of people who are taking prescription drugs for these conditions are staggering. Why do we see this type of stress-related increase? Is our world truly so much worse than it was for a Jewish person during World War II in Germany? What about horrific times of the Christian crusades?

My point in asking the questions is, why the record number of people today who are trapped in a constant state of anxiety? I believe there are many causes for this anxiety-stress syndrome, which we will explore in this chapter.

Please stay with me and allow me to say some things here that may step on some toes. Of course, I am not inferring that all anxiety prescription medications are evil. Also, I am not implying that some people don't genuinely need these medications. My point is the astounding number of Americans who are being prescribed these drugs and then remaining on them for years on end.

Any drug or medication anyone takes for an extended time eventually will experience health consequences. Medications originally intended to use for a limited time often become a crutch resulting in the unfortunate result of addiction. The body then becomes unable to function without the substance.

Are there ways to protect our mental health? The answer is a resounding yes! Are there some people who are predisposed to mental illness? Of course. This chapter is not to diminish or hurt anyone; instead, this chapter's focus is on what can be done to help protect and maintain optimal mental and emotional health.

This best overall method begins by doing everything you can to maintain overall optimum physical health. The most crucial step is to keep emotional illnesses to a minimum by maintaining your overall health.

Maintaining physical health is discussed at length in Section V of this book. When the body is performing correctly, hormones remain in balance, especially the brain hormones that affect mental health and well-being. Make sure and soak in the relevant information in this section of the book.

This best overall method begins by doing everything you can to maintain overall optimum physical health. The most crucial step is to keep emotional illnesses to a minimum by maintaining your overall health.

In addition to good physical health, maintaining optimal emotional health also consists of keeping your spiritual life in balance. Theosynthesis is achieved when the physical, emotional, and spiritual aspects are equally attended. The ability to make a balance in each of these areas can be a challenge.

There are many proactive and practical ways to maintain optimum emotional health. Below are a few suggestions to incorporate into your life to help navigate this stressful and fast-paced life that we live.

- Smile, laugh, and don't take yourself too seriously.

- Lighten up. Allowing yourself to be easily offended causes stress and anxiety. When you learn to let things go, the fear lessens as well.

- Meet your pain where it is. Consistently masking your pain creates a false sense of healing. Pain is designed to let you know that something is wrong. This aspect includes emotional pain. Learning to face your pain rather than escaping it will prevent a possible chemical addiction in the long run.

- Accept yourself. Identify the unique gifts and talents God gave you and embrace them. Ease up on yourself and stop picking out the flaws.

- Do not allow yourself to play the victim card. Own your decisions, choices, and your mistakes.

- Learn to adapt well to growth and change. Change in life is inevitable; therefore, learning to accept it when it occurs and then how to work through it is extremely important.

- Maintain strong personal relationships with others.

- Deepen your walk with Christ.

- Learn to identify the things in your life that are the main stress-producers for you. Understanding what these stressors are can help you learn to handle them effectively and to plan accordingly when you are faced with them.

Some of my final thoughts on the topic of emotional health recognize individuals who suffer from severe psychological issues. This chapter is not intended to cause ill will toward any of these people. The focus of this chapter is to protect and prevent overall mental health issues.

My prayer is for each of you to acquire awareness and understanding. You can proactively do many things to protect your emotional health. Life is going to be tough, and no one escapes emotional pain while on this earth. As you continue your Christian walk, lean on the Father as He is your most significant and most reliable advocate.

Take a moment to list the main stress-producing situations in your life. Pray over your list, and seek God's guidance for ways you can recognize these circumstances. Then ask Him to help you understand effective methods to use to help you navigate the challenges in life.

"A joyful heart is good medicine, but a crushed spirit dries up the bones" (Proverbs 17:22).

THEOSYNTHESIS®

PART VI
UNVEILED MARVELS OF THE UNIVERSE

CHAPTER 31

VIBRATION & FREQUENCY

WAY BACK in Chapter 11, we explored the concept of harnessing God's energy. As we dive into this chapter, we will discover even more of the mechanics involving energy. The study of molecular energy, or vibration, is fascinating, and yet scientists are still learning how the tiny molecules that make up energy move about and function.[1]

For this book, we will not go too deeply into the study of physics. The main goal will be to discuss the fantastic vibrational properties of our world and what this means for us. As we've explored the tremendous structure of living things, it goes without saying that our physical world most definitely has a significant impact on us.

Therefore, understanding the effects that vibration and frequency have on living things makes sense. For instance, when we hear a loud sound or vibration, we can feel it. The sound wave causes molecules to be set into motion, and these vibrations affect the living organisms on Earth.

---

1 Bill Steele, "Physicists Develop Ways to Identify Molecules by Vibrational Signatures," https://www.physics.uci.edu/~wilsonho/N062598.htm, Accessed June 2020.

Vibration is the result of the movement of particles that can be affected by forces such as temperature and speed.[2] Frequency, according to Britannica Encyclopedia, as it refers to physics, is the number of waves that pass a fixed point in a unit of time; it's also, the number of cycles or vibrations undergone during one group of time by a body in a periodic motion. A body in periodic motion is said to have experienced one cycle or one vibration after passing through a series of events or positions and returning to its original state.

A wave then is a disturbance occurring in a rhythmic and organized manner. These vibrations emit frequencies in the form of waves. The different types of waves include sound, light, water, and subatomic waves, along with many others affecting our world in unique ways.

Frequency is a measure of a unit called a Hertz or Hz. Breaking down this unit even further is called a Megahertz or MHz. Now, you've been introduced to the basic knowledge of vibration as it relates to energy. This basic knowledge will help illustrate the Theosynthesis connections as we further explore how things in our unseen world around us operate.

Because God is the Intelligent Designer, He made everything with a specific purpose in mind. He even directed down to the tiniest of detail of molecular vibrations and the frequency of those moving vibrations and how they impact our world. God designed the world in this manner, and it is helpful to learn more about these physical structures and how they make a difference in our lives.

Currently, there are some new and exciting studies called vibrational medicine. These fields of the study believe vibrational medicine

2   Mic Anderson, "Vibration," https://www.britannica.com/science/vibration, April 6, 2020.

or energy medicine is based on the scientific principle that matter vibrates to a specific frequency, thereby, using resonant vibrations, balance or homeostasis, matter, can be restored via these frequencies.[3] This field of the study believes the human body, along with its entire entry field including the physical, emotional, and spiritual elements, can treat dis-orders and dis-ease.

Several researchers and scientists over the years recognized the connection of frequency and the human body. This study is called biofeedback.[4] Biofeedback is a technique used to increase awareness of the body. Functions such as heart rate and respiration are targeted for the patient to control using their mind.

Many athletes use forms of biofeedback to assist them in

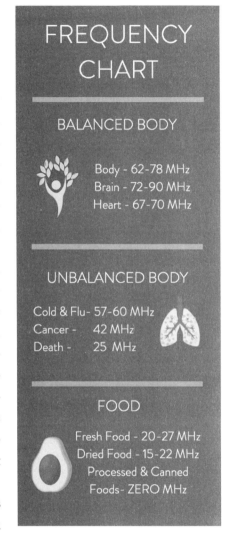

FREQUENCY CHART

BALANCED BODY

Body - 62-78 MHz
Brain - 72-90 MHz
Heart - 67-70 MHz

UNBALANCED BODY

Cold & Flu- 57-60 MHz
Cancer - 42 MHz
Death - 25 MHz

FOOD

Fresh Food - 20-27 MHz
Dried Food - 15-22 MHz
Processed & Canned
Foods- ZERO MHz

3   Kevita Berry, "A Future Perspective for Regenerative Medicine: Understanding the Concept of Vibrational Medicine," https://www.ncbi.nlm.nih.gov/pmc/articles/PMC5859346/, January 5, 2018.

4   Mayo Clinic Staff, "Biofeedback," https://www.mayoclinic.org/tests-procedures/biofeedback/about/pac-20384664, Accessed June 2020.

dealing with healing and pain management. The goal, of course, is to increase performance and maintain optimal health. The results of biofeedback are auspicious, and many are using this form of treatment very successfully.

A biofeedback machine consists of electrical sensors used to measure the frequency of the human body. I first read about biofeedback in the early '80s when I was first out of college. Unfortunately, the critics have squashed these studies down a bit. Early scientists, Claude Bernard in 1865 and Dr. Royal Raymond Rife in the 1920s, created some of the first biofeedback machines.

Most recently in 1992, Bruce Tainio built a biofeedback or frequency machine.[5] His original findings were more specific in identifying a range of frequencies in the human body and plants. He discovered a healthy human body resonates within a frequency range of 62 MHz to 78 MHz.

When our frequency levels in our body drop, imbalances begin. These imbalances, of course, mean the immune system has been compromised. As the frequency level continues to slide, the body becomes increasingly ill. Death begins as the body reaches a frequency level of 25 MHz.

As quantum physics studies continue looking into the behavior of light and matter at the subatomic level, I believe there will be no way to deny the future of vibrational medicine. At some point, modern medicine must come to terms with other forms of dealing with illnesses and embrace perhaps a combination of traditional medical methods with natural methods.

Modern medicine today uses various forms of vibrational frequencies to treat and diagnose disease. An MRI, X-ray, CT scan,

---

5   Bruce Tainio, https://www.tainio.com/about/, Accessed June 2020.

thermography, and radiation are just a few of the modalities using vibration and frequency to diagnose and treat disorders in the body. Vibrational medicine, however, is still in its infancy, and many scholars are curiously seeking more data and information regarding this exciting field of study.

Just as many scholars and people are not open to learning about an intelligent designer named God, it doesn't surprise me at all. Many in the medical industry are not open to some of these new schools of thought and methods in medicine and healing. Science, however, is supposed to remain open to new ways of viewing new schools of thought and not just to say no way.

In my basic understanding of anatomy, physiology, physics, and theology, the more I discover how everything on this earth is connected and how God placed everything we need here to live full, healthy, and prosperous lives. As humans, we have done our part to ruin much of what God perfectly created. We are polluting our water, soil, and air, thus causing disharmony and disease within our bodies.

Vibrational medicine is seeking ways to understand the things that are making us sick via disruption in the natural frequencies within our bodies.[6] When we become ill, our bodies are weakened, and our internal balance or homeostasis levels are off. Wellness and wholeness require these imbalances to be corrected.

The study of vibrational medicine is the focus of what causes energy blocks. Modern medicine recognizes that energy blocks within the body are harmful. Most health-care professionals will not identify an illness as an energy block, and therefore, they will not seek natural methods to help release these blockages.

---

6   Anne Christine Tooley, "Vibrational Energy Medicine Principles," http://www.energyandvibration.com/energymedicine.htm, January 2, 2013.

Instead, they treat illnesses with chemicals that can attack some of the problems, yet these chemicals leave their mark in the body. With synthetic drugs, there are always some side effects to deal with as these chemicals are not naturally derived nor broken down properly in the body. Any substance synthetically made will never be as perfect as something God created and placed on this earth.

Please hear me out on this topic. My intent is not to diminish the medical community in any way. Modern medicine has come a long way since its introduction. Surgeons and highly skilled specialists in medicine save many lives every day. What I am saying is that there are many disciplines of medicine. So it makes sense for us all to be open to these various options and to understand what some might see as old-fashioned or "way out there" might quite possibly be a method offering unconventional cures to some severe diseases and maladies.

I know firsthand how my body is highly sensitive to toxic substances and chemicals. The result has been the life-threatening illnesses I have experienced which have affected my life dramatically. These illnesses have led me on the quest to seek answers and be open to exploring natural modalities. What I term as *natural* only means those items God placed on this earth that are utilized in a way that is as close to how He intended them to be.

It makes no logical sense to me that much of what modern medicine practices are to treat symptoms without achieving a state of being healed. For example, once a person begins taking blood pressure medication, most likely, they will remain on these medications for a lifetime.

Blood pressure must be returned to a correct balance; therefore, improved lifestyle changes must occur. If high blood pressure is due to diseased arteries resulting from years of an unhealthy diet or being overweight, making changes to the food and choosing to begin moving can dramatically affect the blood pressure naturally. The goal should be to start identifying what caused the blood pressure to be out of balance and then seek a regimen to correct the underlying cause.

The question then asks, do natural healing methods work? I believe with an absolute yes, they can. Understanding natural processes and applying them in proper techniques are the key to seeking healing just as they are the goal in modern medicine.

Natural medicine methods, such as pure plant extractions, acupuncture, massage, sound vibration in the form of music, and even crystals, possess healing properties. I know when mentioning crystals, many will say, "Now hold on there, this is getting into some New Age stuff!" Whatever term you want to use for this area is okay; however, the fact is that crystals are used in all sorts of modern equipment.

In addition, do you realize that crystals are found in many items we use every day? Watches, computers, fiber optics, lasers, radios, and even in credit cards? Crystals have the ability within their structure that allows them to store and transmit information very efficiently.

A crystal is formed deep within the earth by intense heat, pressure, and energy. Because of these physical exertions, it makes sense crystals would then contain high vibrational frequencies. We certainly know about uranium and how powerful it is. Therefore, why is it so difficult to accept the power a crystal contains?

Why then do so many doubt a crystal could possess great healing qualities? God created them and placed them on this earth. I don't believe crystals were created to be used only for the world of electronics. Hopefully, many will take an honest and open look at this exciting area of science.

Christians need not fear natural medicine. As I read the book *The Healing Oils of the Bible*, I quote Dr. David Stewart when he asks the question regarding modern medicine: "Can a system that delivers services under the name of 'health care' really deliver health when it fails to acknowledge the very source from which flows all of life and vitality?" Dr. Stewart points out that a vast majority of what we call "health practitioners" are nonbelievers in an Almighty God who is the Ultimate Healer.

Again, I am not saying there are no God-believing doctors out there. Medical schools, however, do not acknowledge God nor recognize His healing methods. Additionally, most medical schools do not focus on natural nutrition methods as a way to heal disease. Many doctors will tell you they took very few courses in nutrition while in medical school. Likewise, they have not studied how natural plants can and do heal illnesses.

When we look back in history, there are many examples of men and women who were called "healers of medicine." These healers used natural plants and herbs to treat illnesses and injuries. They studied various methods to extract the chemical constituents from these plants in a form that could then be used in medicine.

Healers during the biblical times were the priests. People who became sick sought out their priests for healing. These priests were called anointed priests because they were considered to be "set apart" for God's specific purpose.

The first reference of a priest being anointed in the Bible is found in Exodus 29:7: *"Take the anointing oil and anoint him (Aaron) by pouring it on his head."* Later in Leviticus 8:10, it said, *"Moses took the anointing oil and anointed the tabernacle and everything in it, and so consecrated them."* Great detail and information are given in the Bible regarding the anointing of the priesthood. This procedure was essential to God.

As Christians, we are also to be set apart as we are now part of His royal priesthood. To understand the significance of this is to grasp a deeper understanding of our role while on Earth. Because believers are all a part of this royal priesthood, we should take a moment to understand natural laws and understand that God created the things of this earth specifically for us.

In my quest to study and understand natural medicine, the science of essential oils was introduced to me. I have to admit I was skeptical about what I heard out there regarding these oils. Something in me was curious as I sought natural healing methods. I began a quest to find knowledge regarding essential oils with an open mind and with many questions.

What made the most sense to me regarding essential oils is what they are. The term "oil" really should be referred to as a serum. Most of us tend to think of oil as a heavy, greasy solution used for cooking and manufacturing. Fatty acid oils, such as vegetable oils, peanut oils, and olive oils, are what most people identify with when discussing oils in general. The essential oils I am referring to here are the fragrant juices or the aromatic properties of a plant.

These "juices" or serums circulate throughout a plant, which is its lifeblood. They provide plants with the necessary nutrients for survival. The science of adequately extracting these serums from plants is the key to being able to utilize these precious fluids in ways to benefit the body positively.

The chemistry of essential oils shows they are composed of extremely tiny molecules, micro-molecules that are so small they can easily penetrate cells and tissues in living organisms. Because these fluids travel directly into the cellular matrix, these molecules are now free to communicate with the molecules within our bodies to be utilized in extremely efficient ways.

As these essential oil molecules travel throughout each cell, they can bind to cells without leaving a synthetic marker that compromises the cell. This truth means essential oils can heal and correct cells and tissues without compromising the integrity of the cell. Thus, essential oils offer a great alternative source of medicine for those who choose them.

Then why is there such a fuss about essential oils today? The main reason is that essential oils are derived from plants that cannot be patented. Anyone can study plants and herbs and can propagate and harvest them. The large pharmaceutical companies are then not able to control these extracts of oils.

These pharmaceutical companies are controlling and dominant. Just pay attention to the majority of commercials on television these days. Ads for pharmaceutical medications dominate the paid-ad spaces. These drugs are huge moneymakers and big business.

The more I continue to learn the powerful effects of essential oils, the more I understand how the pharmaceutical industry is working desperately to control the companies dedicated to the selling of these oils. The fact is, if I write or tell someone how these oils have helped me in various ways, I must be super careful in making sure I don't use words such as "cure." I can say, "Peppermint oil helps me *feel* better."

Even though restrictions are being placed on holistic methods, there is a trend with people seeking natural remedies. I believe this is the case because for many, they are tired of pumping man-made chemicals into their systems.

The human body is a miraculous machine that is able to heal itself more than we realize. So often, we turn to a drug to help "heal" us and then end up sicker than when we started due to the side effects. Our body will always read synthetic drugs as a foreign substance.

As I have navigated my health issues over the years, I've learned that I do know my own body better than any doctor. Knowing how my body is adversely affected by even the tiniest dosage of medication, I pay attention to the adverse reactions I experience with most drugs and avoid long-term medications.

Each of you also knows your body better than anyone else. If you genuinely desire optimal health and well-being, researching the things God placed on this earth for our health and well-being is encouraged. Doesn't it make sense for there to be many different methods in which healing can be achieved?

I'm sure this diversion into essential oils appears to be somewhat of a rabbit trail since we began this chapter discussing vibration and frequency. There is a connection, I assure you. Please stick with me as I weave these concepts together.

Because essential oils are derived from living plants, it then makes sense these plants would also possess a unique vibrational frequency. This point is why understanding essential oils are important. Why not explore these tiny, aromatic molecules for yourself?

Because oils are incredibly complex in their chemical makeup, one would need a degree in organic chemistry to understand the incredible complexity of each plant. Even with an organic chemistry degree, these chemists are still discovering many amazing complexities within these plants.

An important fact to note, however, is the ability of plant chemistry to be unpredictable. It can vary itself easily. Bacteria are not able to build up a resistance to essential oils. Hmm, this means essential oils can be extremely beneficial in fighting bacterial diseases and then remain active within the cells over time. Now, this is huge news.

Are you being taught this information? Most likely, the answer is no. Again, the large, profitable companies do not want us figuring this out. If the majority of people began lessening the number of pharmaceutical drugs they took and turned to more natural sources, imagine how much money these companies would stand to lose!

Modern antibiotics have been instrumental in treating diseases and have made an enormous impact on our world. However, these drugs must continuously change as bacteria become antibiotic-resistant, and the drugs no longer become effective. Miraculously, essential oils can evolve on their own. This fact points to a great design, wouldn't you say?

The precious drops of essential oils each have their unique vibrational frequency. These frequencies can enter our cells, communicate with them, and then allow the body to receive great benefits from them. Even the tiniest drop of essential oil can have powerful effects.

Let's take a look at the aromatic properties of these essential oils. We can smell because molecules in the air enter the nose and travel to the brain. The part of the brain responsible for smell is also tied to the emotional center. The structure within the brain that houses these functions is called the "amygdala." Here, the brain processes memories and emotions.

This process explains why even a smell can cause a recollection of a specific emotion. Have you ever walked into a place, and the smell of freshly baked bread transported you back in time, perhaps to your grandmother's kitchen? The scent of a particular perfume might bring back memories of a loved one.

The science of smell is big business. Commercials and ads continuously do their best to convince us that these perfumes and scents will attract love, help your home smell clean, and change your mood. The ability to smell is vital.

Because it is scientifically understood, the ability to smell is directly attached to the part of our brain connected to emotion. Then why is the science of aromatherapy not taken seriously by so many in the medical profession? It makes perfect sense that these powerful essential oils can play a crucial role in physical, spiritual, and emotional healing.

Essential oil molecules are loaded with vibrational frequencies of electrically charged subatomic particles. Bruce Tainio also used the machine he developed and designed to measure the frequency rate within essential oils. What he discovered was a frequency level in oils between 52-320 MHz.

The ability to identify various frequencies of specific plants and the oils they produce is instrumental in understanding oils and how they are helpful for various health ailments. Interestingly, rose oil has the highest known frequency of 320 MHz. It's no wonder roses are given as a gift to help raise your spirits. Visually, they are beautiful, and they smell divine. Knowing they contain an extremely high vibrational frequency ties it all together.

There are many studies regarding the effects of negative and positive emotions and what sort of vibrational frequency these emotions produce. In Chapter 31, we discussed the impact of what we think and how these thoughts affect our overall health. Our thoughts are significant. Isn't it fascinating how the type of ideas we produce impacts our overall health?

Therefore, can a particular essential oil with a specific vibrational frequency affect your mood? Absolutely! Aromatherapy is an

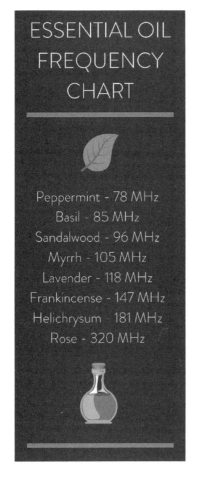

ESSENTIAL OIL FREQUENCY CHART

Peppermint - 78 MHz
Basil - 85 MHz
Sandalwood - 96 MHz
Myrrh - 105 MHz
Lavender - 118 MHz
Frankincense - 147 MHz
Helichrysum - 181 MHz
Rose - 320 MHz

interesting topic, and I encourage you to seek out more information. In the Index at the back of this book, you will find many resources should you choose to explore them.

When we take off the lens of only seeing this world through allopathic science, we can then begin discovering this fantastic world full of natural and miraculous substances that have the power to heal. Allopathic medicine, according to Merriam Webster, is a system of medicine that aims to combat disease by using remedies (such as drugs or surgery) that produce effects that are different from or incompatible with those of the disease being treated.

The Bible contains hundreds of references to oils, balms, fragrances, and incense. Frankincense is referred to numerous times in Scripture. It was one of the oils brought to Baby Jesus. Today, fascinating studies with Frankincense are being tested and are showing very positive results in actually causing cancer cells to explode.[7] This phenomenon is called "apoptosis." This information is revolutionary! Could Frankincense cure cancer? Why not?

---

7   Zawn Villines, "Can Frankincense Treat Cancer?" https://www.medicalnewstoday.com/articles/314366#frankincense-and-cancer, September 24, 2018.

In reading an excerpt on the subject of Frankincense from The National Center for Biotechnology Information, the article entitled "Essential Oils and Their Constituents as Anticancer Agents: A Mechanistic View" states, "Essential oil constituents are potent in cancer prevention and treatment."[8]

I believe with my whole heart that if the science community would begin to study essential oils with an open mind, we might see a treatment for cancer that won't have devastating side effects on the rest of the body. We might look back someday at the way we are treating diseases and wonder why we thought all along a man-made synthetic medicine would be superior to anything God created?

As we will discover in the following chapter, we will continue this discussion of vibrational frequency and how it relates to music. I pray your mind has been opened in seeking and searching God in new ways. It's worth learning all you can about God of the Bible, God, the Creator of Earth, and all of His marvelous creation so that you can appreciate and understand the gifts that are here for us.

Seek Him as you search for answers and increased knowledge. Perhaps, we've allowed ourselves to put more faith into a man-made system called "health care," than into our Almighty God. This question is fundamental and must be considered by every believer.

---

8   Al-Yasiry, Ali & Kiczorowska, Bożena. "Frankincense - therapeutic properties," https://www.researchgate.net/publication/292140720_Frankincense_-_therapeutic_properties, Accessed June 2020.

CHAPTER 32

FREQUENCY IN MUSIC

MUSIC IS and always has been a significant part of life. From biblical times and in our own time today, music has played a vital role in human life. But why do we as humans love music and resonate with it so profoundly? What is it about music that causes us to experience joy, sorrow, passion, and worship?

My journey with music is a limited one. I cannot read one bit of music, yet I appreciate many types. Music can evoke a wide range of emotions.

From our previous chapter regarding vibrational frequency, we know that music also possesses unique vibrational frequencies. Various types of musical instruments all produce individual sounds and resonance. When combined, these instruments become symphonic orchestras of unusual and stimulating sound vibrations.

In the following chapter, we will look closely at the power of words. When a melody is put to words, there is now even more of a powerful connection. There are some songs I hear and am instantly moved to tears. Likewise, let me listen to some good Motown music, and immediately I am transported to the '70s in a flash!

As we continue to explore Theosynthesis and our connection to God, I knew that exploring the phenomena of music was essential to include in this work. Music is a connector for humans because it affects emotions. I believe music is a great tool also connecting us to one another and to God.

Music is a connector for humans because it affects emotions. I believe music is a great tool also connecting us to one another and to God.

Music therapy has begun to emerge as a viable tool for healing. It uses specific tones and a combination of sounds to help people relax. Doctors know that when people relax their minds and bodies, healing can occur more efficiently.

Fascinating studies are being conducted on the positive effect of people who have sustained severe brain injuries. A great in-depth article "How Music Helps to Heal the Injured Brain" by Michael H. Thaut, Ph.D., and Gerald C. McIntosh, M.D, discusses the positive findings in patients who have suffered traumatic brain injuries and when exposed to music therapy, produced positive and dramatic results.[1]

There are also some new studies with Alzheimer patients and music therapy. Many patients who appear to have no recall or memory can suddenly sing a song that has been tucked into their subconscious. Stroke patients may often find they can sing before they are even able to speak.

I don't think anyone would argue the fact that there is something extraordinary about music. Just as in anything else, music can be used for harmful purposes. Flowing, smooth tones have a beautiful rhythm that creates a calming and positive musical effect.

Chaotic, disjointed, loud, and cynical lyrics disrupt sound wavelengths. Music that is disturbing or even painful to the ears would never be the type used in music healing therapy. Music has also been used as a punishment for war prisoners by exposing them to deafening music for hours on end to cause pain.

Then why did God create music? Many, many references to music are in the Bible. Music is discussed in terms of heaven when describing God and is mentioned how music will announce when Jesus returns.

I love this quote by Martin Luther: "Beautiful music is the art of the prophets that can calm the agitations of the soul; it is one of the most magnificent and delightful presents God has given us." These Scriptures below share the importance of music in the Bible.

> "Oh sing to the Lord a new song; sing to the Lord, all the earth!" (Psalm 96:1)

> "Shout joyfully to the LORD, all the earth; Break forth and sing for joy and sing praises" (Psalm 98:4).

> "The Lord your God is with you, He is mighty to save. He will take great delight in you, He will quiet you with His love, He will rejoice over you with singing" (Zephaniah 3:17).

Not only do we worship our Creator in song, but He also sings over us. I can't even imagine this yet, and I look forward to hearing His song over me someday in heaven. The power of music is certainly undeniable.

I am excited to see how the science of music therapy continues to evolve and be developed. It just makes sense that music with its specific vibrational frequencies would also have had an impact on living organisms. It will be interesting to see music incorporated within the medical community in the future as these studies show positive results.

I hope I have the gift of music when I go to heaven. Music is one area I appreciate so much yet have no natural musical talents. I have accepted this fact and have discovered what my unique gifts are and to use them for the kingdom.

In my research regarding music, I stumbled upon a fascinating study performed by a Japanese scientist, Dr. Masaru Emoto. He studied the effects on the water as it was exposed to various sounds that ranged from kind words, classical music, to expressions of anger and hate.[2] The results were captured in his fantastic photographs of water crystals.

What he discovered clearly showed that loving words and beautiful classical music created exquisite water crystals while the words of hate and loud, disorganized music resulted in water crystals reflecting disharmony. These results are quite remarkable and worth looking into more deeply.

In Dr. Emoto's book *Water Crystal Healing*, he says, "In Japanese, we write the word music to mean enjoyment of sounds. What is sound? A sound invariably occurs whenever there is vibration, so we could say that a sound is a vibration. (Although humans only hear sounds generated by vibrations between 15 Hz and 20,000 Hz, which are called audible sounds, all vibrations emit sounds.) Music, then, is an art form through which we experience vibrations, which is energy itself."

---

2   Dr. Masaru Emoto, https://www.masaru-emoto.net/en/, Accessed June 2020.

He also authored the book *The Hidden Message in Water*. Here he writes, "I particularly remember one photograph. It was the most beautiful and delicate crystal that I had so far seen - formed by exposed to words of love and gratitude. It was if the water had rejoiced and celebrated a flower in bloom. It was so beautiful that it changed my life from that moment on."

During this moment, Dr. Emoto recognized that words do matter. If water reacted in this manner, how much more would a living, breathing human body made up of mostly water respond to either positive or negative stimuli and words? What a game-changing concept.

If you are one of those gifted individuals who possess musical abilities, I encourage you to look deeper into the power of music. How does God want you to use these gifts? Protect the artistic skills He has given to you. Let your gift of music glorify the kingdom.

There is so much more to music than this chapter can fully encompass. Music is magical and mysterious. Music isn't like food, water, or oxygen which are essential for sustaining life. But then again, perhaps it is!

CHAPTER 33

POWER IN THE SPOKEN WORD

I HAVE BEEN observing for quite some time that we are losing the gift of communication via the spoken word. I have felt very convicted to include this topic in this book. Isn't it evident by just looking around how everyone has their head buried in a device? Interpersonal, face-to-face communication seems to be taking a back seat to the world of texting, email, and social media posts.

While exploring the topics in the previous chapters on vibrational frequency and music, God has impressed upon me the extreme importance and power of the gift of the spoken word. Having the ability to speak is a unique gift only we as humans possess. Then why on Earth are we dismissing this form of communication today?

Let's go back to the beginning of the Bible in Genesis 1:3, "*And God said, 'Let there be light.'*" The verse doesn't merely say He created the light. The verse clearly says He *spoke* into existence the light.

Therefore, this illustrates that the spoken word is of great importance and has power. Because God created communication, including the spoken word, it makes perfect sense; there is also power in the spoken word. Individually, we each know words matter and affect other people in tremendously personal ways.

Interestingly, the Book of John in the New Testament begins with this concept of the importance of the Word. John 1:1–2, "*In the beginning was the Word, and the Word was with God. He was with God in the beginning.*" Wow, in the beginning was the WORD!

> *The spoken word is of great importance and has power. Because God created communication, including the spoken word, it makes perfect sense; there is also power in the spoken word.*

This reference to "word" actually points to the Word as a being who we know is God. This truth is a vast concept. In digging deeper into the origins of the term "word," the Greek meaning "logos" refers to reasoning and the actual written word.

Another root meaning from the Greek "rhema" refers to the unspoken word. There are many facets and definitions for the term "word" as it relates to a being (God), in referencing a physical thing (written), and then as an unspoken message (God's voice). Just as in other characteristics of God that are depicted in three aspects, isn't it interesting to see the word is no different?

Many people share how they have actually heard God's voice, or they received a message directly from God. Do they genuinely hear an audible voice? Some people say yes, they do. Other's hear God speaking to them within their spirit.

I can attest to hearing God's voice within my inner being. One time in particular, someone very close to me was in a perilous situation.

During the middle of the night, I was awakened very suddenly with an intense sense of urgency to pray for them that very moment.

About a week later, I heard from this person that a horrific incident had occurred near them involving another person being physically harmed. It all happened to them the very night I was awakened. I knew then the inner voice I heard was most definitely God's inaudible voice speaking directly to me and urging me to pray. The older I am and the more in tune I remain with God, the more audibly I hear Him, and I have learned not to question these moments.

As I stay connected and close to God, this is when I have heard Him communicate with me the most. As believers, if we desire to hear from God, we must stay in His Word, remain connected in prayer, and be open to hearing from Him. The connection to the kingdom is critical.

In looking back at the chapters on the vibrational frequency and in music, logically, the spoken word must also have its unique level of vibrational frequency. We know this because the physical characteristics of the spoken word can be tested, heard, and felt. The human voice is quite remarkable when you take a moment to consider this beautiful gift of having the ability to speak words.

This ability to communicate via the spoken word is simply amazing. The anatomy and structure of the human vocal cords and how they vibrate to create sound is an excellent design. The structures that create speech are composed of two folds of a membrane that vibrate as sound waves move over. Therefore, these structures are not cords but folds of membranes.

Because of the way these structures are folded and organized, humans are then able to create a wide range of sounds, tones, and pitch. These sounds provide the basics for all of the human language. As we know, there are many different languages and dialects throughout the world. The spoken word is indeed extraordinarily complex and intriguing.

The purpose of this chapter is to understand the power of the spoken word as it pertains to humans. As a child, I heard the rhyme, "Stick and stones may break my bones, but words will never harm me." As I have experienced many times in my own life, words do matter and do cause harm to others.

Words have the power to hurt, to cause anger and fear. Words also can heal, soothe, create joy, and build up another person. The power of words should be a great reminder to be responsible for the words that come out of our mouths. We should never lose sight of this fact and should never take it lightly.

Scripture contains many verses regarding how we should guard our words and our tongue. These verses should be ingrained within our souls and impressed upon our children. Each of us is entirely responsible for the words we choose to use daily.

I have broken these verses into two different categories of warning words and worthy words.

WARNING WORDS

"Set a guard, O LORD, over my mouth; Keep watch over the door of my lips" (Psalm 141:3).

"A soothing tongue is a tree of life, But perversion in it crushes the spirit" (Proverbs 15:4).

"Death and life are in the power of the tongue, And those who love it will eat its fruit" (Proverbs 18:21).

"*Keep your tongue from evil And your lips from speaking deceit*" (Psalm 34:13).

"*Their tongue is a deadly arrow; It speaks deceit; With his mouth one speaks peace to his neighbor, But inwardly he sets an ambush for him*" (Jeremiah 9:8).

"*A lying tongue hates those it crushes, And a flattering mouth works ruin*" (Proverbs 26:28).

WORTHY WORDS

"*He who restrains his words has knowledge, And he who has a cool spirit is a man of understanding*" (Proverbs 17:27).

"*And at once his mouth was opened and his tongue loosed, and he began to speak in praise of God*" (Luke 1:64).

"*He who restrains his words has knowledge*" (Proverbs 17:27–28).

"*He who guards his mouth and his tongue, Guards his soul from troubles*" (Proverbs 21:23).

"*And my tongue shall declare Your righteousness And Your praise all day long*" (Psalm 35:28).

"*The mouth of the righteous utters wisdom, And his tongue speaks justice*" (Psalm 37:30).

I did not include an exhaustive list of the verses in the Bible regarding how we should use our words but wanted to add a few of them to use as a guide. God wanted us to have many words of wisdom regarding how we use our own words. His Word provides excellent instruction for us on this topic.

When we gain greater respect and understanding of how powerful the spoken word is, this should instill a greater responsibility for what comes out of our mouths. We should be extremely mindful of the type of words we use, which most definitely affects all those we encounter. Words do matter!

Often in my lifetime, I have allowed my words to cause harm to others. I deeply regret the people who have been hurt by what I have carelessly or hurtfully said to them. As I continue to walk with Christ, I pray I will become more and more like Him daily. I ask Him to help me show restraint with my words at all times. I prayerfully seek to be more like Him each day.

Throughout our Christian walk, we have a huge responsibility to use our words carefully and wisely. As we mature in our faith, having the discipline to guard our words is paramount. We learn to control the spewing words of hate, cursing, and words that tear others down or cause emotional harm.

There have been some fascinating studies on the effect words have on people. First, I'll need to refer back to some of the science regarding the human body for just a moment to explain this next section with more clarity and understanding.

The human body is mostly made up of water. Our cells, tissues, and organs are for the most part, water. As humans, we consist of three-quarters water, which is approximately 60% of our makeup. Therefore, water plays a vital role in our general health and well-being.

In reviewing what we discussed in Chapter 31 on vibrational frequency, we know sound has many varying degrees of vibration. Then in Chapter 32, we looked at the vibrational frequency music creates. This information is vital as we move further into our conversation regarding the power of the spoken word.

Each time we open our mouths to speak, we produce sound waves that create a ripple effect. Many scientific experiments have shown the ripple effect of sound waves on water. These studies are fascinating.

A Swiss physician, Dr. Hans Jenny, produced some fascinating studies of this wave phenomena from sounds and words and how they affect water.[1] Down to our cellular level, our cells are comprised of mostly water. Dr. Jenny theorized that sounds and words would then most likely affect the human body itself.

Because our bodies are mostly made of water and have all sorts of fluids flowing through every part of us, it makes perfect sense that sound would also have an impact on us physically. The question is, what kind of impact or effect do various sounds or tones have on the human body?

In the last chapter, we discussed Dr. Masaru Emoto and some of his work. In more of his intriguing studies, he photographed water as it crystallized when frozen. His photographs are quite compelling when you compare the frozen water crystals from words spoken in love with prayers or with beautiful music. Equally as fascinating were the water crystals formed as words of hate, negativity, or heavy metal or fragmented music.

I encourage you to look up these studies and observe some of the pictures. They are truly remarkable. What a perfectly orchestrated world God created for us at every level!

---

1   Hans Jenny, "Cymatics: A Study of Wave Phenomena," http://www.cymatic-source.com/, July 1, 2001.

Because of the design of our water-laden bodies, doesn't it make sense that sounds would also have the same effect down to the cellular level? For me, when I am around someone who spews negativity, I can feel it. I want to run away from it and not be around it in any way.

On the other hand, when exposed to beautiful, soothing music and kind words of affirmation, I experience an entirely different response. Sounds and words are significant not only in what we speak but also in what we allow ourselves to listen to and hear. What you choose to expose yourself to most definitely has an impact on your life.

Think about this: The womb is a sac filled with water housing a developing baby for nine months. It transmits sound through the water very effectively. Mothers are encouraged to play calm music and speak in calming tones to bathe their babies in these loving sound waves.

Because the visual effects of sound vibration on the water can be observed, it also makes sense that a developing fetus's environment that is continuously exposed to shouting, hateful, or harmful words, would have a negative impact. Again, the types of vibrational sound a baby is exposed to should speak volumes to any woman who is pregnant.

Shouldn't we all then consider our words we choose to share? Each of us has a huge responsibility to be cognizant of the types of words we want. Removing yourself from conversations that tear down, insult, and spew hate should be avoided at all costs.

The brain is also bathed in a layer of cerebral fluid. Our hearts, kidneys, liver, stomach, and intestines receive a continual stream of fluids flowing through them at all times. When these fluids are disrupted, the flow is affected, and the health of the organ is altered. Have you ever noticed when you are emotionally upset, how this affect various parts of your body?

With this in mind, retraining your thinking while also protecting what you say could genuinely make a massive difference in your own life. Additionally, imagine the difference it would make to those around you. This realization is enormous. Please take a moment to look up information regarding the impact of positive and negative words on our bodies.

Hopefully, this information has made an impact on you and causes you to evaluate the words, types of music, and the environment you are in daily. Perhaps you've never considered the physical impact within your own body the power of sound has on you. Armed with this knowledge, you can now make positive choices that will impact your life as well as those around you.

Below are some steps to help move you forward in this new thinking. These are practical ways to use this knowledge in a manner that will ultimately help you recognize and utilize the power of words and sound.

Protect what you hear. Think about it. If you are continually listening to negative people, TV shows, movies, or video games that have much violence, you are constantly exposing yourself to these types of sound. Continued exposure to them will have a negative impact and affect what you then choose to share with the world.

Replace the negative things you hear by being selective with what you watch, listen to, and with whom you spend your time. If you have a friend or a group of friends who tend to desire gossip and use ugly, demeaning words, remove yourself from them. Seek out people who are affirming, uplifting, and make you smile.

Set boundaries with the people in your life who tend to be harmful or have a foul mouth. Sometimes we live with these types of people, and it is difficult to remove yourself from them. Having an open and honest discussion with them regarding how this affects you could impact their lives as well. If they choose not to change, you will need to find ways of not allowing their words to impact your life negatively. Many times, just by changing the way you respond to their negativity will begin to cause them to be more mindful of their own words.

Guard your thoughts at all costs. For any words to be formulated verbally, they are first thought within your brain. Retrain your mind to get rid of those words, which are not positively serving you or others. Keep a journal to write down any negative self-talk that may creep into your mind. Often, we become creatures of habit and repeat the same self-deprecating words without really being aware we are even doing this.

Words and thoughts are critical. Every one of us is responsible for what we are choosing to share with the world. God desires us to reflect His character. His character does not include tearing yourself or others down.

Perhaps this is a reminder to makes some changes in your own life. Make today the day you begin letting go of the hurtful words or phrases you have been replaying in your mind for years. Now is the time to renew the way you think.

As we continue to explore Theosynthesis, keeping our secure connection to God does depends on what and how we think. God desires for each of us to have clean thoughts that produce pleasing words. As we walk boldly in this Christian life, every word we choose to use should be considered.

The perfect verse to reflect on as we come to a close on this chapter comes from Romans 12:2: *"Do not be conformed to the pattern of this world, but be transformed by the renewing of your mind."*

What will you do today to renew what you listen to, think, speak, and watch? Make a list and be honest as you assess those things that are not serving you well. As you create your list, think about ways to effectively replace the negative items with more positive and uplifting things in your life.

CHAPTER 34

HEALING THROUGH CONNECTION WITH GOD

IF SOMEONE asked you what the definition of healing is, how would you answer them? I would be inclined to say healing is when a person experiences illness and then becomes well. The dictionary describes healing in the old English term to mean being whole.

Healing then is the process of becoming whole or sound. Any process takes time. Depending on the type of illness or injury will determine how long healing can take. It is also important to note that when a person is working toward "wholeness" or to achieve the Theosynthesis we have been discussing, this too can affect overall healing.

> *Healing then is the process of becoming whole or sound. Any process takes time.*

What I mean by this is taking care of the entire self (mind, body, and spirit). When one part is struggling, healing can be more natural to achieve. However, when more than one part of the whole is sick or damaged, it would make sense to encounter a slower healing process.

Recognizing that when we only address areas such as physical exercise and nutrition in achieving wellness, overall wellness can never be complete without discussing the importance of emotional and spiritual wellness. We must recognize all parts are equal before we can become whole and healthy.

In Chapter 7 regarding a connection with God, we saw the importance of this relationship with Him to our overall well-being. Then why take this concept a step further to understand that healing can and will occur as we connect with God? Does this mean when someone prays for healing, God will always answer them? No, this is not what I am alluding to at all.

Sometimes God heals us when He calls us home to heaven. Yes, this is a difficult concept to accept when we have lost a loved one. For believers, though, joining our Father in heaven is the ultimate healing. We feel the sting of death because we miss having our loved ones physically with us.

Can God then heal us physically? The Bible gives us many, many examples saying, "Yes, God can heal us!" Jesus came down in the flesh in a physical form. Jesus demonstrated that He could perform miracles. Yet even before Christ was born, God showed His people miraculous signs and numerous instances of healing.

In 2 Kings 20, King Hezekiah was very ill and was almost at death's door. Isaiah relayed to him that God said to get his affairs in order as he would not live. Hezekiah poured himself out to the Lord, asking for healing. Isaiah then receives another message from the Lord saying, *"This is what the Lord, the God of your father David says, I have heard your prayer and seen your tears; I will heal you."*

"'But I will restore you to health and heal your wounds,' declares the Lord" (Jeremiah 30:17).

Jesus reads in Luke 4:18, "*'The Spirit of the Lord is on Me, because He has anointed Me to preach good news to the poor. He has sent me to proclaim freedom for the prisoners and recover the sight for the blind, to release the oppressed, to proclaim the year of the Lord's favor.'*"

The connection to God for healing is shown in three different methods from the verses above:

1. HEALING BY CALLING ON THE LORD

2. HEALING AS A PROMISE FROM THE LORD

3. HEALING FROM A PHYSICAL BEING (JESUS)

Types of healing from God include physical, emotional, and spiritual. All three of these are components of our whole selves. As we have seen over and over again during our discussion of Theosynthesis, these three parts of ourselves are equally crucial for wellness.

God can heal us physically from injury or illness, emotionally as we grapple with a difficult situation, and spiritually as we learn to lean on Him rather than on our means. He can use any circumstance in our lives for us to look to Him for comfort, help, and peace. During the times in my life when I was the most challenged in any one of these areas, entirely depending on Him was the only thing that kept me going.

I have often questioned how nonbelievers go through difficult situations with no hope of anything more than beyond this life. I've also heard other believers wondering this as well. No belief or faith in a loving God or of something more than this life would undoubtedly bring a sense of sadness when we die. With the absence of God, we see hopelessness, despair, and frustration rule.

A believer who truly depends on God and has a connection with Him can navigate the harsh, life-altering situations in a completely different manner than the nonbeliever. Although they may still experience fear, a strong faith provides them with hope. Even though the pain of a physical or emotional injury can appear to be too much to handle, a believer still clings to their faith and puts their pain into a perspective that a nonbeliever could never fully understand.

The second time in my life where I was once again told I had a massive tumor in my chest, this one in my lung, I could have easily just given up. The doctors said it didn't look good, and most likely, I would not make it. Sure, I was frightened. As scared as I was, I never, ever blamed God or got mad at Him. Instead, my deep faith in God allowed me to say, "Father, if this is my time, may I die with grace and peace."

On my own, I would have never been able to experience this kind of peace as I walked through this situation in step with the Almighty. During the long recovery and subsequent long rehabilitation from losing a lung, I felt His presence in a way I never had before. There was no doubt my God was right there with me. It certainly was a peace defying any human understanding.

The older I become, the more thankful I am that I walk with God, and He is always with me. With God as my guide, what a comfort it is that I am never alone. The connection I have with the Almighty is genuine, and I pray others in my life and in this world will also experience this same beautiful connection.

If you aren't sure you have this connection with Christ, you can change it this very moment. Jesus said in John 14:6, "*I am the way and the truth and the life. No one comes to the Father except through me.*" If you genuinely believe this and are ready to invite Him into your life, all it takes is a willing heart and your words to Him that you are His. Stop and pray to ask Him to forgive you, and that you are ready to hand over your life to Him and are prepared to trust and follow Him."

It really is this simple. You need no fancy words, no beautiful cathedral, no ceremony, just yourself coming before God and pouring out to Him. It is a lovely way to connect. When you do this, at that very moment, you are now connected to the Almighty. The cord of three strands is not quickly broken as stated in Ecclesiastes 4:12. Prayer binds you to Christ in an intimate and special manner.

If this book has led you to Christ, I would be overjoyed to hear your story. If you feel led to share it with me, my contact information is in the back of the book. I would be delighted to hear from you.

The connection we have to God is powerful. Never doubt He is right there with you and is tethered to you spiritually. This cord is secure, and no man can ever break it. Rest deeply in this knowledge and rejoice.

CHAPTER 35

HEALING
RELATIONSHIPS

PHYSICAL HEALING is easily evident as it can be felt and observed. Human emotional relationships are fragile and can be easily damaged or broken. I am reasonably sure that every person reading this right now has experienced the pain of a broken relationship. This pain can feel as strong as that of a broken bone. Emotional grief and the memory of this pain can often last a lifetime.

We will dig into this chapter to gain an understanding of the importance of healing our relationships with one another. This healing, however, may only be within yourself as you are not in control of how and if the other person receives your forgiveness.

No doubt, relationships are complicated. The word "relationship" means a binding or an attachment. There are many types on human relationships. The primary relationships we are familiar with include friendships, love, coworker, teacher-student, parent-child, sibling, family, social, and casual acquaintances.

Each one of these relationships plays an essential role in our lives and impacts us in many different ways. Some relationships are more comfortable than others, while most relationships are incredibly complex. What we do know is for any relationship to be considered a good one, work needs to be done throughout the process to maintain and protect the bond.

We all know those people who tend to get along with almost everyone. Why is this? The most probable reason is the interpersonal and personality choices of the popular individual. In other words, a friendly person chooses to possess qualities others wish to be around.

People with likability skills typically include the following characteristics:

- They genuinely like other people and show genuine interest in them.
- They are able to cause other's around them to feel good. They exude a positive energy.
- They are trustworthy, honest, and fair.
- They most likely put others ahead of themselves.
- They work to maintain the relationship.

When a mutual affection occurs, we call this a friendship. Friendships are significant relationships throughout our lives. Maintaining those friendships require work.

In my life, I have many different circles of friends. Those from childhood include cousins I am close to, students I have taught, coworkers, classmates, neighbors, church, colleagues, and of course, my "go-to" people. The latter are the circle of friends I know I could call no matter what is going on.

We do know that in order to have friends, you must be able to *be* a friend. I have a quick way to break this down into a visually, easy-to-remember way:

F — FAITHFUL AND FORTHRIGHT. Friendships require loyalty that is constant. Also, being able to be truthful, open, and honest are important factors.

R — RELATIONAL. Being relatable with others means you take the time to get to know someone and can then build a relationship. Relational also means you show genuine interest in the other person to get to know them at a deeper level.

I — INTUITIVE. After getting to know someone on a deeper level, you can then come to understand them. Knowing about someone is one thing; understanding them more intimately is much more complex and takes a lot more time. Being able to instinctively understand another takes time and effort.

E — EMOTIONALLY AVAILABLE. The gift of time spent with another person to truly "hear" them and understand them is critical in a forming deep and lasting friendship. Allowing another person to hear your deepest thoughts, dreams, or fears without judgment is providing them with an emotionally available confidant.

N — NICE. It really is that simple. Being kind and empathetic is the basis for all friendships. Kindness and gratitude arc the two main ingredients for others to feel like they have a true friend.

D — DEPENDABLE. Being reliable and constant are two extremely important attributes of friendship. Friends need to be able to count on one another equally. Of course, there will be times when one friend needs more support. However, a friendship cannot remain one-sided, or it will most likely not last.

Eleanor Roosevelt wrote, "Many people will walk in and out of your life, but only true friends will leave footprints in your heart."

Now that we know what it takes to form and maintain healthy friendships, how do we overcome and heal from a broken one? Unfortunately, many people never recover from a fractured relationship and subsequently live a lifetime of regret and pain. The scar etched into a broken heart can have lasting effects.

> *"Many people will walk in and out of your life, but only true friends will leave footprints in your heart."*
>
> Eleanor Roosevelt

Broken relationships occur when respect has been lost due to hurtful actions or words, misunderstood or absent communication, crossed boundaries, any kind of abuse, loss of trust, or uncontrolled anger that has been lashed out.

Some of my most painful moments in life have been as a result of broken relationships. After a 21-year marriage was over, some of the most physical pain I have ever experienced was felt in my heart. It was the kind of wound that leaves a deep scar.

To overcome this pain, it was up to me to give it to God and allow Him to heal my heart. This process took work on my part. I had to take responsibility for my part, and I needed to learn to forgive. Had I chosen to carry the pain, it would have eventually destroyed me.

Just as an injury to your skin leaves a scar, a painful broken relationship leaves a scar deep within our emotions. Physical scars heal over time. Emotional wounds also can heal. Time is needed while also learning to forgive, letting go, and giving your pain to God. All of these are essential to achieve emotional healing.

Many have been on the receiving end of emotional pain. Likewise, you have no doubt been on the side of the one who has caused emotional harm to another. I too have inflicted psychological pain on others. We are all human, and we make mistakes. Emotional growth and maturity occur when we can face our failures, ask for forgiveness, and then move forward.

Choosing to harbor hate or ill will toward another person ultimately does more harm to you than to the person to whom you are directing the negative emotions. Over time, this negative energy will eat away at you. The result is a sad, angry, caustic individual.

Physiologically, these negative emotions cause your body to dump a boatload of toxic chemicals directly into your system. Naturally, we all have the fight-or-flight chemicals designed to protect us. However, when these chemicals continuously flow through our veins bathing every organ in our bodies over long periods, the result is dis-ease. In other words, your negative energy will eventually make you sick.

Psalm 4:4 says, *"Don't let anger control you."* Control is the keyword. Anger can and will control you and will have detrimental effects if left unattended. God created us with free will and choice. It truly is your own choice to either dwell in anger or hurt or to work through it and learn to let it go.

Most recently, I saw a post from a high school classmate who wrote the following, "I just wish you all had been nice to me in school." She made this comment on a post regarding some of us getting together after 40 years. Sadly, she has been carrying around four decades of hurt feelings.

Emotional and spiritual maturity comes when you can forgive someone even though they were the ones who hurt you. Hanging on to anger will also cause you to be driven by sinful thoughts. The Bible reminds us:

> "Get rid of all bitterness, rage, anger, harsh words, and slander, as well as all types of evil behavior. Instead, be kind to each other, tenderhearted, forgiving one another, just as God through Christ has forgiven you" (Ephesians 4:31–32).

If you are dealing with a broken relationship, whether it is your fault or not, take the first step today toward healing. A great place to begin is before God. Ask Him to help you seek forgiveness from the other person and to seek then to forgive those who have hurt you.

> "For if you forgive men when they sin against you, your heavenly Father will also forgive you" (Matthew 6:14).

Didn't Jesus show us the most amazing act of forgiveness of all? As He hung on that wretched cross, bleeding, in pain, and thoroughly humiliated, He asked God, "Forgive them, for they know not what they are doing" (Luke 23:34). This story is our example as Christians. No matter what, we are commanded to forgive even when it seems impossible to do so.

Prayerfully, go to God right now and ask Him to show you any unforgiveness in your heart. Also, ask Him to show you if there is anyone you have hurt who needs to hear, "I'm sorry. Please forgive me." In seeking to let go of an unforgiving heart, you will find a deep sense of relief as you discard the heavy load of bitterness.

In order to maintain Theosynthesis and an overall wholeness, taking steps to release emotional baggage that is no longer serving you is a must. The mind, body, and spiritual wholeness depends on maintaining a loving, healthy heart and soul. Isn't it time to shed the years of emotional baggage you have been carrying?

CHAPTER 36

HEALING & SELF FORGIVENESS

HAVE YOU ever done something you deeply regretted? Perhaps the moment you said that unkind word or behaved badly or acted sneakily or possibly worse? I bet the answer is a resounding yes. We've all regretted some of the activities we had previously engaged in.

Growth comes when we learn to face our wrongdoings honestly, and then ultimately, forgive ourselves. One of the most concerning issues in our society today is the issue of shame. Guilt is feeling bad for doing something. Shame, on the other hand, involves degrading ourselves, self-criticism, negative self-talk, and feelings of unworthiness.

God does not desire any of us to remain in a state of shame. He does desire us to repent, seek forgiveness, and then move forward. To do this, we must arrive at a point where we are real and honest with ourselves. Sticking our head in the sand over something we are embarrassed about will only prolong the issue.

The results of shame are self-sabotaging behaviors, both to self and others. These actions lead to self-destruction and eventually, self-neglect. None of these behaviors are God-honoring and will ultimately destroy you if not remediated. *God does not desire for us to remain in our shame!*

How, then, do you begin to shake the shame? The list below, while not exhaustive, is an excellent place to start in recognizing shame and then dealing with it effectively. Take this to heart for yourself and also to others who desperately need to hear it.

Recognize the shame, and call it for what it is. If you need to get professional or het pastoral help, do so. Finding someone who can help you remove the shroud of shame is a beautiful first step. These trained individuals can assess the situation outside of yourself and then offer you valuable insight on how to handle it. The result will have the ability to move forward in your life.

Deal with the shame quickly. The longer you avoid facing an awkward situation, the more the emotions will fester and boil. Like an open wound on your skin, shame can become uncomfortable, ugly, and painful. Put your issue out there, and get real with them. Hiding will never correct a shameful situation.

Spend time in prayer. As we have explored in several other sections of this book, there is no doubt that prayer has immense power. God knows every aspect of your heart. You can hide nothing from Him. Therefore, go to Him with your ragged, raw emotions, and give them over to Him. Ask Him for His help. Be open, however, in hearing how He desires you to change.

Make the necessary changes. If you are deep into a shameful situation, you must first recognize and own what you are doing and then make the determination not to repeat the behavior. True repentance, followed by a change in action, is necessary. Saying, "I'm sorry," without a heart, effort, and attitude change means absolutely nothing.

Give yourself a break. Many people live with shame for an entire lifetime. Perhaps the guilt is only for a short season. Whatever it is you are dealing with, face the consequences, and then find a way to move on. Remaining in self-pity is a slime pit in which no one needs to stay.

Do not allow others to shame your game! There will always be unkind people out there who sling around hurtful words. Their end game is shame! Please do not buy into it. Learn to recognize this for what it is—a shame game—and it is not yours to play.

Allowing shame to define your life puts you at risk for not only a sad, lonely, and miserable existence, but also it will also affect your physical health. When all the aspects of our mind, body, and soul are connected to God, we can then begin to experience wholeness. Theosynthetic wellness is the ultimate goal. Likewise, when one part of the body is off and suffering, all of the other parts are affected.

God created your emotional self. The dark forces in this world would love nothing more than to keep people imprisoned by their shame. Your inner light will grow dimmer and dimmer as you remain in an emotionally dark state.

The long-term physical effects of shame are depression and mental illness. Heart conditions, stroke, and cancer are also associated with people who cannot mentally love and accept themselves. Please don't take this as saying all people who have these conditions experienced them due to shame.

The correlation between living in a state of shame with a higher incidence of these types of diseases is quite high. Many medical professionals are just now beginning to understand the connection between emotional and physical self.[1] Hopefully, we will start seeing doctors who can guide their patients to the correct professionals for help rather than just prescribing a pill.

There is plenty of evidence showing that human immune systems are weakened when the body is under stress.[2] A weakened immune system, along with anxiety, releases a toxic chemical dump into the body, which then causes inflammation. Together, this is a double whammy to your overall health and well-being.

I John 1:9 reminds us that *"If we confess our sins, He is faithful and just and will forgive us our sins and purify us from all unrighteousness."*

"Therefore, there is no condemnation for those who are in Christ Jesus, because through Christ Jesus the law of the Spirit of life set me free from the law of sin and death" *(Romans 8:1).*

The words "purification' and "set free" both stand out in these verses. Let's explore what they mean a bit more deeply.

"To be purified" means having contaminants removed or to be cleansed or freed from something. "Set free" means no longer remaining in a state of bondage. In this regard, we are no longer held by the sin and guilt of shame.

Christ didn't die on the cross so you and I could remain on our crosses of shame. He took that away when He willingly died for each

---

1   Madeline R. Vann, MPH, "Connecting the Dots Between Physical and Emotional Health," https://www.everydayhealth.com/emotional-health/connecting-dots.aspx, November 14, 2017.

2   Suzanne C. Segerstrom, Gregory E. Miller, "Psychological Stress and the Human Immune System: A Meta-Analytic Study of 30 Years of Inquiry," https://www.ncbi.nlm.nih.gov/pmc/articles/PMC1361287/, February 6, 2007.

of us. Clinging to bitterness within does not honor what He did for us in any fashion.

Brené Brown is a professor at the University of Houston and the author of the #1 *New York Times* bestseller *Daring Greatly*. She has studied the topic of shame, worthiness, and vulnerability for over a decade. In her book, she digs deeply into the issue of shame.

Brene openly shares some of her shameful memories and experiences and how she learned to overcome them. She says, "It's about the willingness to be imperfect, to be vulnerable. It's about the courage to wake up in the morning and acknowledge that no matter what gets done and what doesn't get done, that I'm enough and that I'm worthy of love, belonging, and joy. Those are irreducible needs for humans."[3]

How beautifully worded! Willing to be imperfect and vulnerable. Yes! Those words sum this point of shame to a T, along with having a willing heart that is "real" and open.

One of my favorite Brene Brown quotes states, "Owning our story and loving ourselves through that process is the bravest thing that we will ever do." Facing ourselves in the mirror and saying, "Get on with it" is one of the best methods to get out of the pit of shame.

> *"Owning our story and loving ourselves through that process is the bravest thing that we will ever do."*
>
> Brené Brown

If you are stuck, seek help. Be open and honest with your trusted friends and family members. They most likely know you are struggling, but they may not know how to help you. Allow those who love and support you to enter into your area of struggle.

---

3 *Brene Brown, Daring Greatly.* Chapter 4.

Change requires turning and going in a different direction and trying a new path rather than remaining in the same routine or pattern. It would be best if you determined to make the decision not to accept the self-doubt or self-pity any longer. You can make all of these are choices right now.

How will your changes look? Effective changes you can implement into your life can have profound and life-altering results. Here are a few helpful tips I have found to climb out of the pit of despair and to overcome rejection, and self-forgiveness:

Never lose your faith. If you are new to the Christian faith or have yet to accept Christ into your life, taking this first step will be the best change you could ever experience. If you are a believer but have doubted if God is there for you, go to Him right now in earnest prayer, and He will meet you right where you are.

Exercise and movement are proven to elevate the mood hormones called endorphins. The brain secretes this amazing chemical during exercise. It bathes your neurotransmitters (the connection point of our nerves' endings), sending a sedative-like happy juice throughout your body.

Take care of yourself. What you place into your body is paramount. If you are depressed, putting toxic chemicals into your system is the last thing you need. Drugs and alcohol deaden the pain. Your pain needs to be dealt with and then released. Also, permit yourself to rest, take a needed break, a vacation, or engage in something as simple as being alone and reading a book.

Learn to recognize the shame symptoms. You know what sets you off. You can feel shame rising within you. If you can learn to avoid the triggers, and this includes people who are shaming you, this is a big step in effectively learning self-forgiveness. You need to avoid the situations and the people who bring about feelings of shame or unworthiness.

Rewrite your story! You can't change the past, but you can certainly make changes for right now and for tomorrow. Do you know people who sound like a broken record? Do they tell you the same problems over and over? They are stuck in their story. Don't let this happen to you, and if it has, stop it! The next page in your book is blank and there for you to pen your next chapter. Decide now to make it a best seller.

I believe this chapter and topic are so vital to the overall message for this book. If you are a parent, be mindful of ways you may be shaming your children. If you are married, stop shaming your spouse. Your words have power, and you are responsible for them.

If you have experienced shame in your life by others, I pray you will take to heart the practical ways you can move out of this trap. Remember, you are the one in control of your shame. Never allow anyone else to take your happiness and joy from you!

THEOSYNTHESIS®

PART VII

UNIQUELY MADE IN THE IMAGE OF GOD

CHAPTER 37

ACCEPTING THE WAY GOD CREATED YOU

COCO CHANNEL quoted, "In order to be irreplaceable, one must be unique." At first glance, I liked the saying. Upon further reflection, however, I realized if I were to rearrange the words a bit, the entire meaning would be changed: "In order to be unique, one must understand how irreplaceable they are."

When we can humbly wrap our minds around the fact that we are perfectly made in God's image and how He created every single fiber of our being, only then can we fully appreciate our traits and characteristics. When we fully understand who we are in His image, we can *then* know we are genuinely irreplaceable.

Have you ever noticed when a trend emerges and how everyone who jumps on that trend begins to look the same? The desired result of being unique is now gone. I remember when the "goth" look became popular years ago. Many students in my classrooms began wearing the all-black, died hair, and dark lipstick.

At first, this style was unique and different. After a while, however, it became redundant as many of the students were dressing the same. What is it about humans that causes us to desire to be like everyone else?

Down at our core, we desire to fit in. Most people don't feel comfortable standing out in a crowd. We want others to like and accept us. Many times in seeking to fit in, we begin to lower our standards and alter the way we look. Sometimes in the process, we lose our own original identity.

What then is our own identity? As Christians, our new identity is in Christ. *"Therefore, if anyone is in Christ, he is a new creation; the old has gone, and the new has come"* (2 Corinthians 5:17). As believers, we now must fully identify and align our new lives as a follower of Jesus.

In this chapter, I would like to explore more deeply the understanding of what a privilege it is to be like Christ and to grasp what so many of us miss, which is how amazing you are just as a perfect God designed you to be. We discussed shame and self-forgiveness in the last chapter; therefore, it is crucial to understand that shame brings a low self-image.

When we don't appreciate ourselves or we continuously degrade ourselves with self-deprecating words, we are telling God that He didn't get us right. Have you ever thought about that? You are telling *the* God of the universe that He messed up!

We also must grasp the fact that God loves each of us unconditionally. He doesn't only love us if we look a certain way or if we are "good." He loves us all of the time. He loves our whole, messy selves. However, you cannot remain in a state of sin, destroying your body or mind. What this means is that you now have a responsibility to live right. He gave you the life you have, and it is now your responsibility to care for it.

How many times have you said, "I hate my nose, my curly hair, my straight hair, my body size?" On and on, we continue to focus on areas of our body we dislike. Often, we obsess tirelessly over these things.

We are in an age where it is becoming more widely acceptable to completely alter our physical facade. Plastic surgery for cosmetic reasons has soared in popularity. People are flocking to surgeons with the sole purpose of changing something they don't like about themselves.

Before you take me out and flog me due to this statement, hear me out. Yes, there is a place for cosmetic surgery. However, when it becomes an obsession to completely alter and change everything about how you look, there might quite possibly be a much deeper psychological issue happening.

Today, I see women and men who go from a small number of cosmetic surgery alterations to over-the-top changes that are garish and harsh. The more surgeries upon surgeries continue to create a face or body that no longer represents their original look in any way.

As I age, sure, I look in the mirror and see many changes happening quickly. The hair is graying, the lines of aging are appearing, and the skin is not as taut as it once was. If I spend my time flipping through the latest fashion magazines, I might at times feel a twinge of desire to look like I did in my '20s.

Those twinges don't last long as I have learned to accept myself where I am right now. I'm 60 years old. My body has been through a lot. Gravity is real. Aging is real. Yet I do not allow myself to throw a pity party because I am aging.

As a Christian, I have learned to thank Him for the body and physical form He gave me. Growing up, I was teased because I was too thin. I was a scrawny little thing with bones sticking out everywhere. As I have grown older, that skinny frame has changed over time for sure. Additionally, this body of mine has also served me well over the years.

Rather than lament over what I no longer have, I have placed my focus on living a life that is pleasing to our Father. To do this, it includes taking care of this precious body He gave me. In Chapter 24, we discussed the importance of caring for the body as a temple before God. Go back and reread it if you need to.

When we truly understand and appreciate that God created us exactly the way He desired, only then can we begin to accept the way we are. When we reach this mature way of thinking, guess what? No longer will you place all of the pressure upon yourself to look a certain way.

This doesn't mean you can allow yourself to become a blob who doesn't care how they look but that you can't be overly obsessed with the concept of being perfect. I desire to look my best and to present my best self to the world. I can do this, however, without the pressure to become someone I am not.

After numerous surgeries to my upper torso over the years, there are many wicked scars as reminders of those trials. These surgeries were not cosmetic; they were life-saving. I've had to learn to look at these scars with appreciation rather than seeing them as ugly. I've often said that my back now looks like a Texas roadmap.

In the same way, the belly that was once flat is not so flat anymore. "Thank You, Lord, for the belly that allowed me to bring two beautiful children into the world." For the aging lines on my face and neck, I can sincerely say, "Thank You, Lord, for allowing me to live 60 years. Thank you for the laughter in my life, which helped create those lines."

Looking back upon my teenage years, I am thankful for those people in my life who built me up to focus on what I could do to impact this life. Rather than seeking what the world could do for me, this perspective helped keep the focus off of myself and onto bigger things. This attitude has directed me on a path of adventure and without self-imposed limitations.

What if each of us genuinely believed and acted on John F. Kennedy's famous quote: "Ask not what your country can do for you, ask what you can do for your county"? I would bet we would see a lot more people working together for one cause rather than being a fragmented country with individuals all seeking what is best for them.

I mention this because at the root of not being able to accept oneself lies the fundamental flaw of selfishness. Ouch! I know that steps on some toes, so stay with me a moment. When we spend valuable time worrying about ourselves, we are spending less time reflecting on the things in this life that go far beyond self.

"Woe to you, scribes and Pharisees, hypocrites! For you cleanse the outside of the cup and dish, but inside they are full of extortion and self-indulgence" (Matthew 23:25). Here, Jesus is clearly saying not to spend all that time fussing about how you look on the outside. Instead, focus on the inside because this is what needs attention.

If you struggle with a lack of self-acceptance, take a moment to do an honest evaluation before the Lord of the things you don't like about yourself. Ask Him to help you focus on the good qualities you do possess. Learn to embrace what you might see as imperfections. Look through His perfect eyes rather than through your critical lens.

Remember, in Chapter 33; we explored the importance of words and thoughts. They do indeed, make a difference. If you are in a constant state of negative self-talk, you are wiring your brain to believe those things. You become what you think and what you say.

Philippians 4:8 says, "*Finally, brothers and sisters, whatever is true, whatever is noble, whatever is right, whatever is pure, whatever is lovely, whatever is admirable—if anything is excellent or praiseworthy—think about such things.*" Paul is teaching us where our focus needs to be placed.

Truth, nobility, alignment with God, pure, lovely, admirable, excellent, and praiseworthy. Now, these are unique words of affirmation. Maybe you should start placing your name into these Scripture verses to see yourself as God sees you. *You* are right, pure, lovely, admirable, excellent, and praiseworthy.

When you catch yourself even thinking negative statements about yourself, focus on why you may be saying these things. If you don't like the fact that you are overweight, make the necessary adjustments to lose weight. If you don't believe you are smart, start reading and studying. You are in charge of you.

When you rewire your thought process from the negative to the positive, you will be amazed at the changes in yourself, and others will also begin to see these changes too. You are a new creation. Embrace this imperfect yet perfect self you are. You are the only *you*.

CHAPTER 38

DNA: GOD'S FINGERPRINT

DNA, the genetic fingerprint of life, is one of those discoveries I know God smiles about as we discover the perfection of this design. The more I have learned about the complexity of living things, the more solidified I am in knowing we have an intelligent designer, and His name is God! As we explore the fantastic structure of DNA, I believe you will also understand what a tremendous creation we are.

We will need to geek-out a little to understand what DNA is and why this unseen structure lies within every cell of every living thing. I'll do my best to unfold this surprising discovery in a way that will challenge your thinking. I also aim to show you what a truly remarkable design is hidden deep within our cells.

Here is a quick mini-lesson:

DNA stands for deoxyribonucleic acid, which is a self-replicating material present in nearly all living organisms. It contains the genetic code of information for the cells. This genetic material is contained within the cell in the center of the cell called the nucleus.

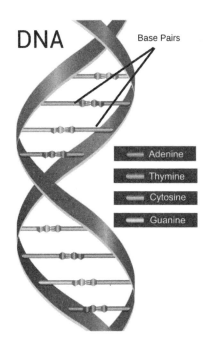

It is also found within another cellular organelle, the mitochondria.[1]

When DNA was discovered in the '50s by Dr. Watson and Dr. Crick, it opened an entirely new way of thinking and thus created a new study called genetics. In reality, this is still a relatively new field of study. Every day, discoveries are being uncovered.

Basically, within the DNA, there are two outer strands composed of sugars and phosphates. Within these two strands are four chemical bases, Adenine, Thymine, Cytosine, and Guanine, arranged in base pairs. Adenine is paired with Thymine, and Cytosine is paired with Guanine. Now, we have a structure that resembles a ladder. This double helix, as it is referred to, is twisted tightly, allowing for more information to be placed within a smaller space.

If you unravel a ball of yarn, soon you will have a big pile of string. The smaller you can wind up the thread, the smaller and tighter it becomes. Therefore, for the DNA to have the ability to store every bit of genetic code into the tiny nucleus of a cell, it must be wound very tightly.

---

1   Michael W. Davidson, "Mitochondria," https://micro.magnet.fsu.edu/cells/mitochondria/mitochondria.html, November 13, 2015.

What is truly remarkable about this double helix strand is the bases at the junction where these base pairs meet. At these junctions, the strands can unzip from one another and replicate itself. This action becomes a template for the new strand of DNA. This process blows my mind when I think of how perfectly designed this is.

Again, as science has shown, there is nothing simple at all about this structure of DNA. This fantastic ball of DNA structures forms the entire informational code for every cell of our body. The complexity of DNA points to an intelligent designer. Every ounce of logic within my brain cannot accept the theory that all of life emerged over millions or billions of years and randomly arranged to create the extreme complexity of living things.

I don't believe anyone would hesitate to question if the informational system for a computer just randomly formed over time. That hypothesis would undoubtedly cause others to question your sanity. Logic points to an intelligent person who created and input the correct information and codes to generate the computer itself.

But what about our computer information system which is in the form of DNA? Our genetic code is super-complicated and contains more information than any computer code ever could. Think about this the next time someone suggests that all of life just organized itself over millions and millions of years. This fact is more ludicrous to me than believing a machine formed on its own.

To understand this more visually, one human alone consists of approximately 100 trillion cells. Within each of these cells, DNA is continuously manufactured. A lot is going on in that cell. The DNA is only one part of it Many other complex structures are within each cell. Each cellular structure is also unique in its design and function.

These four bases along the DNA chain create a specific code. For instance, ATC TGA GGA AAT GAC CAG. This code is not random. It is highly accurate to instruct the cell what it is supposed to do. There is no way this could have evolved randomly. Only an intelligent designer could have created this unique structure.

Inside every cell within your body are three billion of these letter combinations. Now, take that number and multiply it by the number of cells at 100 trillion. That is many zeros and more than my finite human brain can grasp.

A gene is a segment of the DNA that expresses specific information to a living organism. It tells the cell what its function is. Will the cell become skin, cardiac, brain, bone, or nerve cells? Each strand of DNA for these tissues has precise instructions for its function and purpose. Genes provide living beings with their individual coded instruction guide. This instruction manual tells the living thing the features it will exhibit.

We now have the basic anatomy of DNA, and hopefully, a better understanding of its purpose. This fantastic fact would help you also grasp the concept of what an amazing being you are and that a perfect and all-knowing God designed you. All the way down to your DNA level, you are unique and perfectly designed.

I believe the fingerprint of God is within our DNA. His utterly complex structure determines who we are and how we will look. Our DNA also determines our personalities. Because God said He made us in His image, I would like to expand on the topic a bit further.

If we are created in God's image, He wired us. Therefore, I believe the verse in Genesis 1:27, "in His image," means God is woven and wired into our entire being. Psalm 139:16 says, *"For You formed my inward parts; You knitted me together in my mother's womb."* Notice the word "knitted" used in this verse. Just like the strand of DNA that is woven together, doesn't it make sense that God, our Designer, has His fingerprints all over it?

Being made in God's own image has vast implications on this topic of Theosynthesis. Our perfect God created and designed us to *know* Him. Because we are wired down at the DNA level, man is wired to seek Him. In His infinite wisdom, however, He allows us to come to that decision on our own.

Therefore, if we are wired to know Him, and we choose to ignore Him or to deny His existence because we are wired to know God, there now becomes a void within our lives. When we deny our Creator, we are out of balance. We do not have Theosynthesis, and due to our wiring, we live our lives trying desperately to fill that "God-void" or "God-gap" with other things.

When this concept came to me, it simply took my breath away. It makes perfect sense. None of this has to be complicated. *We* choose to make it complicated.

Also, think about the verse from Psalm 139:13 that describes being woven in our mother's womb. When this verse was written, DNA was not even a blip on anyone's map. This fact alone is mind-blowing. Therefore, the more science glimpses into His fantastic design, the more I believe we can see and recognize His fingerprint.

My mind is blown. Each of us is uniquely made in our Father's image down to the tiniest unit of life, the cell. Each one of us carries His DNA within us!

CHAPTER 39

EPIGENETICS

NOW THAT WE have a basic understanding regarding DNA, we can now explore a bit more deeply into the study of changes occurring within organisms over time. These changes cause the DNA to modify how genes are expressed. This fact means the genes can turn on or off. The codes are read by the cells.

The study of Epigenetics is truly an emerging science that is important for us to understand as we continue to appreciate the incredible complexities within us.[1] As the study of epigenetics has been uncovered, what we eat, how we sleep, and the things we are exposed to each affect us down at the genetic level.

Back in 1942, a few scientists began looking into the hypothesis of combing the study of genetics with developmental biology. Later, this study evolved into the study of epigenetics. This word comes from the Greek word "epigenesis," meaning the development of something.

These studies lost their steam, and as recently as the 1990s, slowly emerged as science has a renewed interest in the area. Genes were

---

1   https://www.whatisepigenetics.com/what-is-epigenetics/, September 1, 2019.

expressed in various ways while not altering the genetic code itself; instead, they showed "heritable" changes. These were changes we inherited from our ancestors that include the connection between cancer, immune disorders, mental disorders, the environment, and right down to the daily choices we make as humans.

As scientists put on a new lens of thinking, this field is gaining interest as they explore lifestyle choices and how we live, which directly affect changes within our genes. This discovery truly changes the picture when we begin to understand that our bodies are not our own. The realization that what we do and how we treat our bodies can and will affect the next generation at the genetic level.

Stop and think about this for a moment. What you eat, the chemicals you are exposed to, and even anger, emotional distress, and overall stress do affect each of us at the DNA level. Therefore, how you care for your body and how you protect your health is paramount in what you pass genetically to the next generation.

Each one of us is responsible for this life we have been given. Additionally, this means we are also responsible for the next generation should we decide to have children. When I hear people say, "This is my body, and I can do to it whatever I want with it" causes me to cringe inside. The teenage and young adult years are infamous for experimenting with drugs and alcohol with no regard for future damage to their bodies nor the next generation.

When we elect to dump toxic chemicals into our system via diet and pharmaceuticals, we are altering the ways our genes are expressed. Our lifestyle choices do indeed affect more than just yourself. Therefore, we have a significant and responsible role to play as we begin to understand this fully.

1 Corinthians 6:19–20, "*Do you not know that your bodies are temples of the Holy Spirit, who is in you, whom you have received from God? You are not your own; you were bought at a price. Therefore, honor God with your bodies.*" This verse sums it up, and God directs us that we do not own our bodies, that this body and life we have been given are not free. Yes, we each have the responsibility to care for it.

Section V of this book goes into great detail regarding the proper care of our bodies. If you haven't already, I encourage you to visit that section and perhaps reread those chapters. When we honestly appreciate the gift we have been given with this life, we then begin to view things in a different light.

I was fortunate to hear a talk by Dr. Tom Reed in The Woodlands, Texas, a few years ago on the topic of epigenetics. He explained that because of the toxins in our environment and in the type of food we consume, genetic changes are most definitely occurring. He made the analogy that these toxins create epigenetic tags or markers within our genes.

Cigarette smoke, for example, can cause over 50,000 gene mutations. The evidence supports syndromes in newborn infants as a result of the effects of smoking, alcohol, and drug use. Epigenetic studies show that not only are these babies affected at birth, but also, many will have lifelong genetic alterations because of these choices by one or both of the parents and even earlier generations.

Therefore, before becoming pregnant, what your mother ate, drank, and exposed herself to as well what the biological father and grandparents did, generationally affects the child. Women are not the only responsible parties here. As we know, a sperm and an egg create life. Therefore, both the male and female genes are passed via these sex cells, ultimately affecting a fetus.

If you then choose to destroy your own body with toxic substances, you must understand that should you decide to have children someday, this decision will have consequences on your children and subsequent generations. Interestingly, this study of epigenetics is finding that these tags or markers can be carried into three to five generations. This result is called epigenetic inheritance.[2]

Isn't this interesting as we view the verse, "*Yet He does not leave the guilty unpunished; He punishes the children and their children for the sin of the fathers to the third and fourth generation*" (Exodus 34:7). We can see the connection regarding sin (adverse personal choices) affecting to the third and fourth generations.

However you wish to view this, the evidence is quite compelling. Many cannot wrap their minds around a loving God who punishes those who have yet to be born. Yet how can we have a loving God who isn't just? Justice must follow sin. If sin is left on its own without consequences, then there is no justice.

God isn't the one to blame for these injustices. We alone must understand when sin entered the world, corruption, disease, and crimes also began. We must stop blaming God for the choices we make, which ultimately affect the following generations.

God didn't intend for His children to be affected by sin this way when He created the world. As we know in Genesis, when He created man and allowed him to have free will, everything changed. When man willingly disobeyed God, sin and its consequences entered the world.

"*But if they confess their iniquity and the iniquity of their fathers...if then their uncircumcised heart is humbled and they make amends for their*

---

2 Martin I. Lind,Foteini Spagopoulou, "Evolutionary Consequences of Epigenetic Inheritance," https://www.nature.com/articles/s41437-018-0113-y, August 2017.

iniquity, then I will remember my covenant with Jacob" (Leviticus 26:40–42). Thankfully, we have a loving God who sent a way for us to receive redemption of sin.

> *"For God did not send His Son into the world to condemn the world, but to save the world through Him. Whoever believes in Him is not condemned, but whoever does not believe stands condemned because they have not believed in the name of God's one and only Son" (John 3:17–18).*

God lovingly became flesh in the form of Jesus, who came down to this crazy earth to dwell among us. Then of His own free will, He became the living sacrifice to redeem His people who willingly choose to follow Him. God desires that we embrace and honor this life He has given to us. We then have a considerable responsibility to Him and the following generations.

What we do in our lifetime does indeed leave a genetic footprint. Have you ever wondered where musical talent seems to emerge naturally in some people? Or perhaps, a predisposition to superior athletic or academic skills? DNA imprinting is stamped into our genetics from many generations back.

Even more exciting are the studies now being done regarding DNA memory. Is it possible to have a memory from our ancestors who lived generations before us? The scientific evidence is showing just that. Science is proving what they call "intergenerational imprinting" of passing down the genetic footprint of traumatic experiences, illnesses, and toxins.[3]

---

3   Anne C Ferguson-Smith, Deborah Bourc'his, "The Discovery and Importance of Genomic Imprinting," https://www.ncbi.nlm.nih.gov/pmc/articles/PMC6197852/, October 22, 2018.

I find this quite exciting as this explains déjà vu or what some people call a past life or reincarnation. As a Christian, reincarnation doesn't add up. We have already explored how each of us is amazing and unique. There is nothing in Scripture supporting God requiring our souls to enter and re-entering various life forms or time frames. Hebrews 9:27 reminds us that people are destined to die once.

DNA memory or imprinting then provides a very logical explanation for those who know they have been someplace before or perhaps have a memory of something from long ago that suddenly manifests in their mind. This truth makes so much sense that these memories are real memories buried deep within our genetic makeup. I am anxious to learn more about this school of thought as more scientists begin to research this area.

One recent study found that the descendants of Holocaust survivors have lower levels of the hormone cortisol.[4] This chemical in our system helps us during traumatic situations. Therefore, DNA imprinting and memory of high cortisol levels have been passed to the next generations causing those individuals to be less able to handle stress.

To sum up this chapter, the main message is what we choose to fuel our bodies with and how we treat our bodies impacts not only ourselves but also the following generations. We each do have a responsibility then to honor our bodies as not unto ourselves.

I find it no accident that the word "generations" contains the word *gene* or the word *genesis*. The Greek word "genos' means offspring or race. As you move forward in your life, take heart that you are entirely made down to your genes. Your genetic imprint is carried on well after you are gone from this earth.

---

4   Tori Rodriguez, "Descendants of Holocaust Survivors Have Altered Stress Hormones," https://www.scientificamerican.com/article/descendants-of-holocaust-survivors-have-altered-stress-hormones/, March 1, 2015.

I urge you to dig into this topic more deeply if you find it interesting. I am looking forward to the future of more discoveries in the study of epigenetics. I believe it will provide us with just another glimpse into the mind of God. Don't you know He is smiling as He watches these discoveries unfold and how they point directly to Him?

CHAPTER 40

BEING WHOLE

AS WE CONTINUE exploring Theosynthesis, we now culminate into the question of what all of this means? We know when we choose to ignore God or to deny Him altogether, we are no longer whole. Only true wholeness can be experienced when we connect the mind, body, and spirit to His triune self—the Father, the Son, and the Holy Spirit.

One definition in the Merriam-Webster Dictionary defines *wholeness* as "the state of being unbroken or undamaged." When we experience wholeness by connecting to Almighty God, our broken and damaged lives can then begin to be repaired and renewed. We receive this promise directly from Him.

Wholeness, however, does not happen immediately. Just as in nature, living organisms are born or grown from one cell into millions of cells, this process does not happen overnight. Humans begin life from a single cell to a complete human in just nine months. To me, this is mind-boggling.

Being a woman who had the privilege of giving birth twice, being able to experience this process caused me to appreciate the enormity of the event entirely. As a biologist with an understanding of how an egg and a sperm join to create a baby, the actual process is nothing short of miraculous.

When we become Christians and give our lives to Christ, He says we are a new creation *"Therefore, if anyone is in Christ, the new creation has come: The old has gone, the new is here"* (2 Corinthians 5:17). As a "new creation," old habits and behaviors do not instantly change.

Just as the single cell of the human egg began to divide and multiply, it changed and increased over those nine months. Upon accepting Christ, our faith is new, and we are now promised salvation. We are saved from our sins and are promised eternal life with Him.

The cycle of life from conception, development, childhood, adulthood, and then death is the cycle of life. As we begin our new walk as a new creation, we now enter into the cycle of Theosynthesis. We experience this Theosynthetic completeness as we shed the old and start walking in our new life with Christ. We now have an incredible connection to the Almighty Himself.

These steps in moving from a new Christian into spiritual maturity will take a lifetime. You are now on a Theosynthesis journey as you never stop growing as a true Christian in your faith walk. How you choose to become depends on what you do with your time, your talents, your gifts, and your service to Christ. It also depends on spending time with Him and getting to know Him.

THE THEOSYNTHESIS JOURNEY AND CYCLE TO WHOLENESS

PHYSICAL BIRTH — This is the moment you arrive as an infant

SALVATION — Accepting Jesus into your heart, you are now delivered from sin and the eternal separation from God. The Holy Spirit enters our lives and guides us as we move closer to God daily.

SANCTIFICATION — This journey is the process in which we are slowly transformed into the image of Christ as we spend time with Him, study His Word, and follow His commands.

"And we, who with unveiled faces all reflect the Lord's glory, and are being transformed into His likeness with ever-increasing glory, which comes from the Lord, who is the Spirit" (2 Corinthians 3:18).

GLORIFICATION — This part is the work of God as we continue to sanctify our old selves and trust in Him with our whole lives. The focus on the blessed hope of Christ will eventually bring us into full and final glory with the Lord.

I have given them the glory that You gave Me, that they may be one as We are One" (John 17:22).

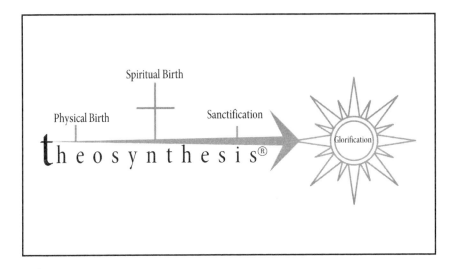

In a message to the American Association of Christian Counselors, John Piper indicates that "praising the glory of God's grace is the apex of (mental health) human wholeness."[1] Without God, we are never fully complete. There is a God-gap!

We must continuously pursue God as we run toward the goal of glorification. I pray you will never cease in running the good race toward our loving Father. May you feel His sanctifying love within every fiber of your being.

"And let us run with perseverance the race marked out for us" *(Hebrews 12:2).*

---

1   John Piper, "Beholding Glory and Becoming Whole: Seeing and Savoring God as the Heart of Mental Health," https://www.desiringgod.org/messages/beholding-glory-and-becoming-whole, September 6, 2009.

CHAPTER 41

WHAT'S MISSING IN YOUR LIFE?

IF YOU HAVE stayed with this book to these last few chapters, I hope it has given you a lot to process. We've discussed everything from cellular biology to neuroscience and many topics in between. This stunningly beautiful and complex world in which we live continues to intrigue my mind and inspire me.

As you have reflected on the various areas of your life, the question now lies in what might be missing. Do you feel complete, or are you seeking, questioning, or feeling unsettled? Even as a born-again Christian, we will encounter trouble, temptations, doubt, and fear. Thankfully, this physical realm we live in while on Earth is only a temporary home.

> *"For our light and momentary troubles are achieving for us an eternal glory that far outweighs them all. So we fix our eyes not on what is seen, but on what is unseen. For what is seen is temporary, but what is unseen is eternal" (2 Corinthians 4:17–18).*

For humans to understand the balance of life and to experience Theosynthesis, it is necessary to grasp all of the parts indeed that make up the whole. Health, mental wellness, and connecting with God and with others are all aspects of being whole. Perhaps though, there is still that area within you that needs to be filled and completed.

This missing piece could be as simple as putting others first, along with overall kindness. When we understand Jesus's central message, which was love, isn't that what He meant, that to enjoy fullness in this life, we must take care of one another and love one another deeply?

Love is such a misused word and has lost some of its original intended meaning. "Oh, I love that movie" or "I love chocolate" are ways we use love to describe the things we like. Love can also be a feeling associated with sexual desire.

Let's take a quick look at the word "love." The Greeks defined seven different types of love.

1. **EROS** — passionate, romantic, or sexual love

2. **PHILIA** — love associated with a good friend

3. **STORGE** — love between a parent and their children or other family members

4. **AGAPE** — the universal love of God

5. **LUDUS** — playful or flirtatious, uncommitted love

6. **PRAGMA** — practical love of duty, work, community

7. **PHILAUTIA** — self-love

Agape love is in the center and is where all love should begin and where all other love should emanate.

Most likely, we have all experienced all of these types of love sometime within our lives. Aside from agape love, many of the other six types can be misused, abused, withheld, or even worshipped. When love is used as a weapon, it can hurt.

This thought reminds me of the song sung by Nazareth:[1] The song tells the story of love hurting and leaving scars. How true these words are when you have experienced the pain resulting from love.

Most of us can relate to love actually causing us intense pain. We have been so wounded from a love experience that we'll never fully recover. Often, this can cause us to distrust and disable us to trust love again. Wounded love takes time to heal. The heart wound will indeed heal, especially when we go back to the pure love of God.

Interestingly in the Bible, the first mention of love is found in Genesis 22:2 where God says, "*Take your son whom you love, your only son Isaac, whom you love.*" In John 3:16, Jesus says, "*For God so loved the world that He gave His one and only Son, that whoever believes in Him shall not perish but have eternal life.*"

These beautiful verses show a Father's love for his child or children. In the absence of love, the Bible would be fruitless. Jesus is God's gift of love to humanity. When we grasp the importance of this love, we can then begin to sincerely and wholeheartedly love others.

Being loved by God is something too many people miss. When I experienced the pain of divorce and felt unloved, He reminded me in such a loving way that I was not only loved, but I was beloved! He then led me to this verse found in Deuteronomy 33:12:

---

1   Dan McCafferty, "Love Hurts," https://www.imdb.com/title/tt8846460/, 1974.

"Let the beloved of the Lord rest secure in him, for He shields him all day long, and the one the Lord loves rests between His shoulders."

The word "beloved" jumped right off of the page in the Bible and was seared into my heart. At that moment, I experienced agape love like never before. He was saying to me, "I know you have been hurt and feel unloved, but I love you so much, and you are My beloved!" This verse was the first step in my heart healing and has been a beautiful reminder to me over the years.

When the Sadducees and the Pharisees were questioning Jesus, they asked Him which was the greatest commandment in the Law. Jesus replied in Matthew 22:36–40,

"'Love the Lord your God with all your heart and with all your soul and with all your mind.' This is the first and greatest commandment. And the second is like it: 'Love your neighbor as yourself.' All the Law and the Prophets hang on these two commandments."

The Apostle Paul wrote one of the most essential and beautiful chapters in the Bible on love in 1 Corinthians 13:

"If I speak in the tongues of men or of angels, but do not have love, I am only a resounding gong or a clanging cymbal. 2 If I have the gift of prophecy and can fathom all mysteries and all knowledge, and if I have a faith that can move mountains, but do not have love, I am nothing. 3 If I give all I possess to the poor and give over my body to hardship that I may boast, but do not have love, I gain nothing.

*4 **Love** is patient, love is kind. It does not envy, it does not boast, it is not proud. 5 It does not dishonor others, it is not self-seeking, it is not easily angered, it keeps no record of wrongs. 6 **Love** does not delight in evil but rejoices with the truth. 7 It always protects, always trusts, always hopes, always perseveres.*

*8 **Love** never fails. But where there are prophecies, they will cease; where there are tongues, they will be stilled; where there is knowledge, it will pass away. 9 For we know in part and we prophesy in part, 10 but when completeness comes, what is in part disappears. 11 When I was a child, I talked like a child, I thought like a child, I reasoned like a child. When I became a man, I put the ways of childhood behind me. 12 For now we see only a reflection as in a mirror; then we shall see face to face. Now I know in part; then I shall know fully, even as I am fully known.*

*13 And now these three remain: faith, hope and love. But the greatest of these is **love**."*

We hear this chapter quoted a lot, especially at weddings. The depth of love discussed in this chapter is rich and deep, So I want to dissect it a bit to assist in an even deeper understanding.

I see four major principals or sections of these verses:

SECTION I: (VERSES 1–3) VALUELESS LOVE

In the absence of love, we can possess various talents and gifts, but if we lack the main ingredient, which is love, these mean absolutely nothing.

SECTION II: (VERSES 4–7) VIRTUE OF LOVE

These verses describe what love should look like and also

what it should not look like. This is the instructional section of the chapter.

SECTION III: (VERSES 8–12) VAIN LOVE

Man can possess knowledge, but without love, it is meaningless.

SECTION IV: (VERSE 13) VICTORIOUS LOVE

This is the main message of faith, hope, and love whereas love is defined as the greatest.

Paul very clearly provides us with this excellent guide about love. What a perfect reminder for us to never lose sight of these descriptions. He then ends his lesson on love, teaching us very clearly that we can possess faith and hope, yet love is the main point.

As you put into practice the many of the principles of Theosynthesis, know that if all of this knowledge you have learned doesn't reflect into love, it is all meaningless. We as Christians must radiate God's love and share it with those around us.

CHAPTER 42

DISCOVERING YOUR MISSING PEACE

PEACE IS something I know I crave. In Chapter 25, we looked into the importance of rest and of being still. The peace we will explore in this chapter is about an inner peace that provides you with tranquility and calmness.

"And the peace of God, which transcends all understanding, will guard your hearts and your minds in Christ Jesus" (Philippians 4:7).

The peace of God! Here we see this kind of peace being unlike any other we will experience on our own. Just as the word "love" can have many different meanings, peace is the same way.

The four types of peace can be defined as:

CALMNESS — a peace of tranquility, being clear in mind and emotions

CONSCIOUS — a peace of understanding and of being aware

CONFIDENT — a peace of being secure and safe

COMFORT — a peace of relaxation, rest, and ease of spirit

Here we see four different descriptions of peace. When God says His peace that transcends or exceeds our understanding, this is the peace that can only come from Him. Imagine being able to possess the four types of peace throughout your life.

The people I know who have learned true peace within their spirit exude a calmness; enjoy a confident, inner security; and can find comfort within their mind, body, and spirit. Being around people like this is enjoyable. Their spirit of peace can be felt.

As we know, achieving this kind of peace is easier said than done. The world continues to nip at our heels with responsibilities, demands, and difficulties. Often, the problems we experience rob us of our joy and our peace. We must then find a way back to the missing peace.

As you continue to connect with God and work to remain in a state of Theosynthesis, peace can be found even when things are upside down in your life. The spirit of this entire book is to be able to find a balance. Allow me to share the word "balance" as an easy way to be reminded of how to find your missing peace.

BREATHE: Breathing is typically an effortless experience. Those who have breathing difficulties understand its importance when they are unable to take in the needed oxygen properly. Have you ever noticed when you are under stress, you can find yourself holding your breath?

Learning to breathe deeply is an excellent method to relieve stress. Deep breathing calms the nervous system and delivers more oxygen to your brain and cells. When you find you are under tremendous strain, take a moment to breathe slowly and deeply.

Another aspect of breathing is merely taking a moment to stop and smell the roses. Don't get so busy in your life that you miss the moments in life. Many of us are missing so much simply because we are whizzing through this life at warp speed. Learn to minimize the minutia to maximize the moments.

ATTITUDE: While a former high school educator, I witnessed a lot of bad attitudes from some of my students. Teenagers, as we know, can be known to have less than lovely manners. Your attitude indeed says a lot about you.

Attitude is a choice every day. No matter what is going on in your life, it is never all right to have a selfish, mean-spirited, or hateful attitude. These behaviors do affect the people around you.

As this relates to peace, having a sour attitude will most certainly not provide you with a peaceful spirit. Those who choose to hang on to a nasty attitude will not experience the peace that transcends all understanding.

LOVE: Go back and reread the chapter above as it examines the many types of love. To discover God's peace, you must have a love for yourself and others.

ACCEPTANCE: Feeling accepted refers to the acceptance by others or within society. The acceptance that provides inner peace is when we can accept who you are and where you are right now. Always wishing for different circumstances in life will lead you down a path of never having enough.

NURTURE: Caring for your mind, body, and spirit is essential to finding peace. Make sure you value yourself enough to nurture each of these areas.

CALM: Jesus gave us a great visual of remaining calm in a storm. In Mark 4:39, Jesus was awakened while He and His disciples were out at sea in a boat. As a storm whipped up, the disciples became frightened. He (Jesus) got up, rebuked the wind and said to the waves, "*Quiet! Be still!*" Then the wind died down and it was completely calm.

Learning to calm your spirit will help you when the storms of life come along. As Christians, we possess the genuine knowledge that He dwells within us, which gives us such an assurance of peace. Sure, we will experience scary things in this life. Yet as we learn to remain calm and lean on Him, we will experience this incredible peace from Him.

ENERGY: Protecting your energy is vital in experiencing peace. When you are rested, healthy, and well, it is easier to experience peace. Peaceful individuals radiate energy unlike anyone else.

Your words, your actions, and your thoughts affect your inner peace. Be mindful as you evaluate the self-talk running through your mind and of the words you choose to speak. Words and thoughts have energy. Choose your words carefully as they will bring joy and peace.

Are you missing your peace? It's there for you, my friend. Seek out God's guidance earnestly and ask Him to show you His unique peace.

"Your faith has saved you; now go in peace" (Luke 7:50).

CHAPTER 43

MOVING FORWARD

I AM STILL in amazement of what God has shown me as I have obediently walked with Him through this process of writing this book. Since the inception of Theosynthesis, I have wrestled with what God wanted me to include in this book.

Nothing we learn in life is meaningful if we don't do something with the new information given to us. As we move forward, equipped with fresh thoughts, encouragement, and perhaps a little butt-kicking, we now need to be responsible with *what* we have learned.

A book like this is certainly not one that you picked up and read through like a novel. I hope you have made notes, used a highlighter to remember specific information that inspired you, and have grown in your faith and understanding of our great God. Also, I hope this will serve as a guide that you can come back to time and again.

Like any good teacher, as we close, I would like to provide you with some helpful tips and suggestions as you prayerfully evaluate where you are right now and where you are headed in your spiritual journey. If we don't use the information God is showing us, it is indeed wasted.

Suggestions for moving forward with Theosynthesis:

1. Grab a journal and write down your "aha moments" from each chapter.

2. Make a list of lessons or changes you plan on incorporating into your life as you move forward.

3. Decide what you are leaving behind. What things are no longer serving you and can be thrown out?

4. Don't make excuses for things God has shown you to do in your life. If He has given you those thoughts and ideas, He has entrusted them to you. Therefore, you have no excuse, so just get busy!

Here are eight strategies I call my eight *Ps*" as you digest this information:

PRAY: Ask God to clearly show you what you need to let go of and what you need to hold onto.

PLAN: To utilize any information, you need a plan of action. Journaling, spending time in earnest Bible study, research, and read. Then watch His plans unfold before you.

PREPARE: Be realistic in setting your goals. When you have appropriately prepared by being prayed up, fed adequately, and are in the right mindset, watch out!

PRIORITIZE: What is vital in your life, and what are the time-wasters? Decide on those things you need to get done and organize them.

PRACTICE: Do you need to make some lifestyle changes to live a balanced life? It takes time and much practice to make it happen.

PERSEVERE: Never give up what God has instructed you to do. When He convicts you of something, He will give you the help when you call out to Him earnestly.

PROGRESS: Celebrate your successes no matter how tiny they may seem to you at the time. Moving forward means progressing ahead.

PUT INTO ACTION: Today is the day to begin whatever it is you need to do. A plan without action is just a bunch of wishful thinking.

Jesus desires for us to move forward with Him as we become more and more like Him. As we entrust every aspect of our lives to Him, He equips us. Hold on to Him and allow His love and grace to pick you up wherever you are. He is right there waiting just for you.

> "Let your eyes look straight ahead; fix your gaze directly before you (Proverbs 4:25).

> "'For I know the plans I have for you,' declares the Lord, 'plans to prosper you and not to harm you, plans to give you hope and a future'" (Jeremiah 29:11).

"For since the creation of the world God's invisible qualities—his eternal power and divine nature—have been clearly seen, being understood from what has been made, so that people are without excuse." (Romans 1:20).

"Being confident of this, that he who began a good work in you will carry it on to completion until the day of Christ Jesus" (Philippians 1:6).

"I press on toward the goal to win the prize for which God has called me heavenward in Christ Jesus" (Philippians 3:14).

ALLOWING THEOSYNTHESIS TO CHANGE YOUR LIFE

THIS JOURNEY of discovering Theosynthesis that God invited me to walk with Him on has been a wonderful experience. As the concept was birthed, outlined, and written, God has been faithful to walk ahead of me. His guidance and assurance have remained steadfast.

As I wrestled with being called to do this work, God has lovingly opened door after door and gently pushed me through them. I clearly remember arguing with the Almighty that He had indeed chosen the wrong person to complete this work. I pointed out that I only had a bachelor's degree, was not a theologian, nor a "big" name.

How patient He was and how wrong I was. During the past few years, doors have been flung open to complete my master's and my doctoral degrees, both in theology. And this book was accepted as my dissertation toward the doctoral program.

I believe in a big God. He did choose me, and He paved the way to debunk my original arguments. We are always more capable of doing much more than we can even imagine, especially when we move over and let Him take control.

I pray this book has opened your mind in new ways. More importantly, I pray that you have grown closer to our Lord. Finally, I pray you have gained a renewed desire to dig into His Word like never before.

We are all on a journey in this life, and as believers, we are to participate in the harvest. Never has there been a better time than now to be equipped and ready to share God with others. He has a plan for each of us to share in this good news!

I leave you with a challenge. Has God laid in you an idea, ministry need, or perhaps a work that He has planned precisely for you? Take those ideas and lay them at His feet with an open heart. He will show you what to do and how to accomplish His work through you.

Never doubt for a moment that whatever He is calling you to do, He entrusted this task and will enable you to complete the work. Just trust in Him and allow Him to do mighty things in and through your life.

Be blessed and fruitful, and remember to live this day and every day in His fullness!

BIBLIOGRAPHY

al Absi, Mustafa. *The Neuroscience of Pain, Stress, and Emotion.* New York: Academic Press, 2016.

Adams, Mike. *The Hidden Toxins Lurking in Your Foods.* Dallas: BenBella Books, Inc., 2016.

Booker, Richard. *Miracle of the Scarlet Thread.* Shippensburg: Destiny Image, Inc., 2017.

Brown, Brene. *Daring Greatly.* London: Penguin Books, 2013.

Cain, Michael Lee. Campbell, Neil A. Minorsky, Peter V. Reece, Jane B. Urry, Lisa A. Wasserman, Steven Alexander. *Campbell's Biology.* London: Pearson Education, Inc., 2015.

Chambers. Oswald. *My Utmost for His Highest: Classic Edition.* Grand Rapids: Our Daily Bread Publishing, 2011.

Chapian, Marie. *Quiet Prayer: The Hidden Purpose and Power of Christian Meditation.* Nashville: Emanate Books, 2019.

Emoto, Masaru. *The Hidden Message in Water*. New York: Beyond Words Publishing, Inc., 2001.

Engel, Jonathan. *Fat Nation: A History of Obesity in America*. New York: Rowman & Littlefield, 2018.

Frisch, Joachim. *Biophotons*. London: Springer Netherlands, 2013.

Fosha, Diana. Siegel, Daniel J. Solomon, Marion. *The Healing Power of Emotion*. New York: W.W. Norton & Company, Inc., 2009.

Geisler, Norman L. *Baker Encyclopedia of Christian Apologetics*. Grand Rapids: Baker Publishing Group. 1999.

Gerber, Richard. *Practical Guide to Vibrational Medicine*. New York: HarperCollins Publishers, 2000.

Horst, Gert J. *The Nervous System and the Heart*. Totowa: Humana Press, 2000.

Lamonthe, Lori. *Kirlian Effect*. Mineral Bluff: FutureCyle Press, 2017.

Karsdal, Morten A. *Biochemistry of Collagens, Laminins and Elastin*, London: Academic Press, 2016.

Malkmus, George H. *The Hallelujah Diet*, Shippensburg: Destiny Image Publishers, 2006:

Masters, Maxwell Tylden. *Botany for Beginners*. Sacramento: Creative Media Partners, 2019.

Mercola, Joseph. *Take Control of Your Health*. Chicago: Mercola, 2007.

Moreland, J.P. *Love Your God with All Your Mind*. Carol Stream: Tyndale House Publisher, 2009.

Packer, J.L. *Knowing God*. Downers Grove: Imprint of InterVarsity Press, 1973.

Packer, Lyn. *Co-Creating with God*. Maricopa: XP Publishing, 2017.

Palacios, Danielo. *Epigenetics and Regeneration*. London: Academic Press, 2019.

Pascal, Blaise. *Thoughts, Letters, and Minor Works*. New York: Cosimo Classics, 2007.

Prieve, John. *Big Pharma*. Baltimore: PublishAmerica, 2006.

Safari, Jonathan D. *Refuting Evolution*. Green Forest: Masters Books, 1999.

Salasnich, Luca. *Quantum Physics of Light and Matter*. Gewebestrasse: Springer International Publishing, 2017.

Scott, Woltman. *Liquid Crystals: Frontiers in Biomedical Applications*. Hackensack: World Scientific Publishing Company, 2007.

Senn, Frank C. *Christian Worship and Its Cultural Setting*. Eugene: Wipf & Stock Publishers, 2004.

Spurgeon, Charles. *The Essential Works of Charles Spurgeon*.

Uhrichville: Barbour Publishing, Inc., 2009.

Stanley, Charles F. *Living in the Power of the Holy Spirit.* Nashville: Thomas Nelson Publishing, 2005.

Tyrrell, Michael S. *The Sound of Healing.* Brandon: Barton Publishing, 2014.

Ulloa-Aguirre, Alfredo. *Cellular Endocrinology in Health and Disease.* Amsterdam: Elsevier, 2014.

Warren, Rick. *The Purpose Driven Life.* Grand Rapids: Zondervan, 2002.

Watson, James D. *DNA, the Secret of Life.* New York: Knopf Doubleday Publishing Group, 2009.

Young, Gary D., *Seed to Seal.* Lehi: Young Living Oils, 2017.

ANCILLARY
STUDY GUIDE

THE SECOND PHASE of this book will be about creating an ancillary study guide. I believe this book can be taught as an educational course.

The guide will follow the outline from the books and will contain:

1. Exploratory questions
2. Fact questions
3. Inductive questions
4. Personal reflection questions
5. Encouragement to dig deeper

This booklet will complement the overall experience of Theosynthesis as the topic is quite expansive.

RESOURCE GUIDE

BELOW ARE a couple of the resources I mentioned in this book or that I believe in and use personally. Should you wish to simply order without joining any type of organization, products may be ordered without requiring a membership.

Because I have researched everything that I use on a daily basis, these products are those I highly recommend and endorse. Perhaps you too will enjoy them.

—Dr. Paula McDonald

YOUNG LIVING ESSENTIAL OILS
https://www.youngliving.com/apps/enrollment/step/1

ARBONNE — HEALTHY LIVING TO IMPROVE MIND, BODY AND SKIN
https://www.arbonne.com/pws/paulalmcdonald/store/AMUS/default.aspx

TOPICAL INDEX

SCRIPTURAL INDEX

1 Corinthians 1:10, 13, 18,
24, 2:4-5, 16, 5:4, 6:14, 19-20,
13:1-13
2 Corinthians 1:19-20, 2:4-5,
3:18, 4:17-18, 5:17, 6:7, 12:9, 13:4
Galatians 2:20, 5:22-34
Ephesians 1:19, 2:10, 3:16, 20,
4:22-24, 31-32, 6:10
Philippians 1:6, 2:9-11, 3:14, 21,
4:6, 7, 8, 13, 22, 31-32
Colossians 1:11, 15-20, 29, 2:12,
3:23-24
1 Thessalonians 1:5
2 Thessalonians 1:9
2 Timothy 1:8
Hebrews 1:3, 5:7, 6:5, 8:10, 9:27,
12:2
James 1:5-8, 25, 4:8
1 Peter 1:5, 2:21, 3:22, 4:10
2 Peter 1:16
1 John 1:9
Revelation 1:8, 3:15-16, 4:11,
5:9, 11:17, 17:9, 22

ABOUT THE AUTHOR

AUTHOR, speaker, educator, business owner, and community leader, Dr. Paula McDonald combines years of professional experience with a passion for learning.

Aside from numerous on-going projects, in her spare time, Dr. McDonald can be found enjoying her grandchildren, staying active, and striving to seek balance in her life.

Having moved back to her hometown of Granbury, Texas, Paula and her husband and son are enjoying living the dream in a small, Texas town.